Reforming Occupational Licensing in the US

Clifford Winston
Editor

Reforming Occupational Licensing in the US

Reducing Social Costs and Increasing Social Benefits in the Legal, Medical, and Financial Services Professions

Editor
Clifford Winston
Economic Studies Program
Brookings Institution
Washington, DC, USA

ISBN 978-3-031-74348-1   ISBN 978-3-031-74349-8 (eBook)
https://doi.org/10.1007/978-3-031-74349-8

© The Editor(s) (if applicable) and The Author(s), under exclusive license to Springer Nature Switzerland AG 2024

This work is subject to copyright. All rights are solely and exclusively licensed by the Publisher, whether the whole or part of the material is concerned, specifically the rights of translation, reprinting, reuse of illustrations, recitation, broadcasting, reproduction on microfilms or in any other physical way, and transmission or information storage and retrieval, electronic adaptation, computer software, or by similar or dissimilar methodology now known or hereafter developed.

The use of general descriptive names, registered names, trademarks, service marks, etc. in this publication does not imply, even in the absence of a specific statement, that such names are exempt from the relevant protective laws and regulations and therefore free for general use.

The publisher, the authors and the editors are safe to assume that the advice and information in this book are believed to be true and accurate at the date of publication. Neither the publisher nor the authors or the editors give a warranty, expressed or implied, with respect to the material contained herein or for any errors or omissions that may have been made. The publisher remains neutral with regard to jurisdictional claims in published maps and institutional affiliations.

This Palgrave Macmillan imprint is published by the registered company Springer Nature Switzerland AG

The registered company address is: Gewerbestrasse 11, 6330 Cham, Switzerland

If disposing of this product, please recycle the paper.

Contents

1 Introduction — 1
Clifford Winston

2 Can Deregulating the Legal Industry Significantly Benefit American Society? — 7
Clifford Winston

3 Is Deregulating the Medical Profession Just What the Doctor Ordered? — 77
Conor Norris, Robert Orr, and Edward Timmons

4 Balancing Flexibility and Integrity: Reforming Licensing in Accounting and Financial Advising — 111
John M. Barrios

5 Conclusions — 149
Clifford Winston

Index — 155

List of Contributors

John M. Barrios Yale SOM, New Haven, Conn, USA

Conor Norris West Virginia University, Morgantown, WV, USA

Robert Orr Niskanen Center, Washington DC, USA

Edward Timmons West Virginia University, Morgantown, WV, USA

Clifford Winston Economic Studies Program, Brookings Institution, Washington, DC, USA

LIST OF FIGURES

Chapter 4

Fig. 1	States adopting the 150-hour rule	125
Fig. 2	Demeaned number of candidates taking the CPA exam in event-time relative to the rule year	127

LIST OF TABLES

Chapter 4

Table 1	Summary of proposed licensing reforms in accounting	132
Table 2	Summary of proposed licensing reforms in finance	140

CHAPTER 1

Introduction

Clifford Winston

Abstract This chapter outlines the contents of the book, which assess the case for reforming occupational licensing in the legal, medical, and finance professions. It previews that occupational licensing of all these professions in the form of training and certification requirements has created barriers to entry for workers entering the profession. Those barriers can limit competition, raise service costs, and restrict consumer access to essential services. At the same time, consumers have incurred these costs without being adequately protected from incompetent or unscrupulous service providers.

Keywords Occupational licensing · Legal profession · Medical profession · Finance profession

Occupational licensing, a form of government regulation that requires people to obtain a license to work in a particular profession, has become a mainstay of the US labor market. In recent decades, nearly 30 percent

---

C. Winston (✉)
Economic Studies Program, Brookings Institution, Washington, DC, USA
e-mail: CWINSTON@brookings.edu

© The Author(s), under exclusive license to Springer Nature Switzerland AG 2024
C. Winston (ed.), *Reforming Occupational Licensing in the US*,
https://doi.org/10.1007/978-3-031-74349-8_1

of workers have required a license from a government agency to perform their jobs legally compared with less than 5 percent of workers in the early 1950s (Kleiner and Kreuger 2013). A wide range of professional service workers require a license, including lawyers, doctors, and accountants, as well as florists, hairdressers, physical therapists, and plumbers.

The primary theoretical justification for occupational licensing lies in addressing the information asymmetry between service providers and consumers. It posits that potential consumers often lack the information and knowledge to judge the competence of a service provider; necessitating a regulatory system that ensures that customers are served by people who have received adequate training and certification in their profession. In practice, this often requires prospective practitioners to complete their training by obtaining a degree from a professional school's multiyear program as well as being required to obtain certification by passing a state's examination for a license to practice their profession legally. Generally, professional associations approve the training and regulations of practitioners' behavior, while licenses, which convey a legal authority to work in an occupation, are awarded by a federal, state, or local government agency.

Notwithstanding the alleged benefits of occupational licensing, its training and certification requirements amount to entry barriers to the profession, which may limit competition and raise service costs, and limit consumers' access to essential services. This skepticism is not new. Economists' opposition to actions that restrict competition can be traced to Adam Smith's *Wealth of Nations* (1776), where he pointed out that when people of the same trade are brought together, the conservation ends in "some contrivance to raise prices." In *Capitalism and Freedom*, Milton Friedman (1962) characterized occupational licensing, which protects people of the same trade from competition, as a way to raise prices by limiting the supply of workers in specific occupations.

Contemporary empirical studies further underscore the various inefficiencies caused by occupation licensing including: (1) costs to consumers attributable to fewer service workers in low and moderate-income professions (Flanders and Roth 2017; Han and Kleiner 2016), and in the leading professions, including law (Winston and Karpilow 2016), medicine (Timmons, Bayne, and Norris 2020), eyecare (Mills and Timmons 2018), and finance (Barrios 2022); (2) higher prices of licensed services to consumers (Kleiner 2015); (3) reductions in employment among workers seeking employment in licensed services (Kleiner and

Soltas 2023); (4) impediments to the interstate movement of workers in a profession that requires occupational licensing, which can increase unemployment (Johnson and Kleiner 2020), and (5) prohibitions on ex-offenders from working in a profession that requires a license (Kleiner and Vorotnikov 2018).

In response to arguments that occupational licensing provides social benefits, two compelling pieces of evidence question the most important benefits that are claimed. First, empirical research has found that occupational licensing has not protected consumers from incompetent and unscrupulous service providers. For example, Winston and Karpilow (2016) argue that lawyers who have graduated from law school and passed a state bar examination often fail to provide adequate service to their clients. Second, advances in information technology have significantly reduced the problem facing consumers of imperfect information about the quality of a service provider by making available on public forums information about a provider's competence and reputation based on objective evaluations provided by third parties and on customers' reports of their experiences with the provider.

While it may be easy to criticize a government policy, such as occupational licensing, it is not obvious how occupational licensing should be reformed to improve social welfare. Given that occupational licensing is a form of government regulation, a reasonable starting point for exploring its reform is to consider the broader history of regulatory changes of US industries, which focused on partial or full industry deregulation. Past experiences with industry deregulation revealed that regulations often create hidden costs, which become apparent only after the regulations are removed. Furthermore, those experiences showed that deregulation can provide benefits that are much greater than originally anticipated (Winston 1993, 1998).

Economic regulation of US industries was often driven by concerns over the market failure that may arise from natural monopolies, whereas occupational licensing seeks to address concerns over the market failure that may arise from imperfect, or more precisely, asymmetric information (Winston 2021). However, the questionable benefits of occupational licensing lead the authors in this volume to focus on its costs, which stem from entry barriers that restrict competition, raise prices, and reduce the availability of service to American consumers. Accordingly, by curtailing occupational licensing, we can allow market forces to spur competition while playing a central role to ensure the competence and quality of service providers and to improve the nation's welfare.

The shift in policy could reveal that existing licensing regulations impose greater costs than previously understood and that those costs have been suppressing significant benefits that a more open market could produce. Recently, industry associations and practitioners in some occupations have voiced a desire to expand public access to their services by policy reforms that could increase the supply of practitioners. Despite this interest, however, policymakers have yet to propose, let alone implement, reforms to eliminate or significantly reduce the entry barriers to professional services.

Given the evidence of both occupational licensing's extensive costs and questionable benefits and the possibility that greater reliance on market forces could improve on occupational licensing's shortcomings, this book aims to propose constructive reforms and assess their effects on the leading professions of law, medicine, and finance.

We confine our discussion to those professions for three reasons. First, all occupations differ in important ways, so nuanced reform of occupational licensing for each profession is necessary to produce the best social outcome, which in turn calls for an occupation-specific analysis that clarifies a reform's objective and its likely effects on the welfare of members of society who may be affected by changes in the occupation's licensing. Second, ample evidence exists that occupational licensing has significantly reduced the public's access to those professions' valuable services. Finally, the leading professions have a large impact on the quality of life in the United States by: (1) enabling people to settle disputes peacefully and promoting social justice; (2) helping people to care for and improve their body's health and wellness; and (3) enhancing the efficiency and fairness of capital markets. Thus, in addition to expanding access to those professions' services, appropriate licensing reforms could benefit the entire nation by improving public policies, reducing healthcare costs, and promoting more efficient capital markets.

The three chapters that follow carefully examine the costs and alleged benefits of current occupational licensing policies toward the legal, medical, and financial professions and propose and justify licensing reforms for lawyers, physicians, accountants, and financial advisors. A common theme of the chapters is that after identifying and discussing the significant costs of current occupational licensing policies, they recommend practical reforms that entail greater reliance on market forces, which could produce extensive benefits by reducing licensing's costs without compromising service quality. The final chapter synthesizes the analyses and the policy recommendations.

REFERENCES

Barrios, John M. 2022. Occupational Licensing and Accountant Quality: Evidence from the 150-Hour Rule. *Journal of Accounting Research* 60 (1): 3–43.

Flanders, Will, and Collin Roth. 2017. Land of the Free? 50 State Study on How Professional Licensing Laws Lead to Fewer Jobs. *Wisconsin Institute for Law & Liberty*, October. www.will-law.org/wp-content/uploads/2017/10/final.pdf.

Friedman, Milton. 1962. *Capitalism and Freedom*. Chicago: University of Chicago Press.

Han, Suyoun, and Morris M. Kleiner. 2016. Analyzing the Influence of Occupational Licensing Duration on Labor Market Outcomes. *NBER Working Paper 22810* (November).

Johnson, Janna E., and Morris M. Kleiner. 2020. Is Occupational Licensing a Barrier to Interstate Migration? *American Economic Journal: Economic Policy* 12 (August): 347–373.

Kleiner, Morris M. 2015. Reforming Occupational Licensing Policies. Hamilton Project Discussion Paper 2015-01, January, Brookings Institution.

Kleiner, Morris M., and Alan B. Krueger. 2013. Analyzing the Extent and Influence of Occupational Licensing on the Labor Market. *Journal of Labor Economics* 31 (April/2): S173–S202.

Kleiner, Morris M., and Evan J. Soltas. 2023. A Welfare Analysis of Occupational Licensing in U.S. States. *Review of Economic Studies* 90 (5): 2481–2516.

Kleiner, Morris, and Evgeny S. Vorotnikov. 2018. *At What Cost? State and National Estimates of the Cost of Occupational Licensing*. Institute for Justice. https://ij.org/wp-content/uploads/2018/11/Licensure_Report_WEB.pdf.

Mills, Anna, and Edward J. Timmons. 2018. Bringing the Effects of Occupational Licensing into Focus: Optician Licensing in the United States. *Eastern Economic Journal* 44 (January): 69–83.

Smith, Adam. 1776. *An Inquiry into the Nature and Causes of the Wealth of Nations*. W. Strahan and T. Cadell.

Timmons, Edward J., Ethan Bayne, and Conor Norris. 2020. A Primer on Emergency Occupational Licensing Reforms for Combating Covid-19, 26. Mercatus Policy Brief: George Mason University, March.

Winston, Clifford. 1993. Economic Deregulation: Days of Reckoning for Microeconomists. *Journal of Economic Literature* 31: 1263–1291.

Winston, Clifford. 1998. U.S. Industry Adjustment to Economic Deregulation. *Journal of Economic Perspectives* 12 (Summer): 89–110.

Winston, Clifford. 2021. *Gaining Ground: Markets Helping Government.* Washington, DC: Brookings Institution Press.

Winston, Clifford, and Quentin Karpilow. 2016. Should the US Eliminate Entry Barriers to the Practice of Law? Perspectives Shaped by Industry Deregulation. *American Economic Review Papers and Proceedings* 106 (May): 171–176.

CHAPTER 2

Can Deregulating the Legal Industry Significantly Benefit American Society?

Clifford Winston

Abstract The legal industry's self-regulation creates entry barriers for firms and people who seek to provide legal services and for institutions that seek to educate lawyers. In this chapter, I provide a prospective assessment of whether deregulating the legal industry could benefit American society. I argue that deregulation would benefit consumers by allowing new entry of firms and individual lawyers who would reduce prices and increase the availability of legal services. I also argue that deregulation of legal education would result in lawyers being less intellectually siloed, which could provide enormous social benefits by exposing lawyers to

---

I am especially grateful to Kyle Rozema for his careful and thorough review of this chapter. I also am grateful to David Burk, Dennis Carlton, Robert Crandall, David Grubb, Philip Hanspach, Rohan Pavuluri, Peter Schuck, Timothy Taylor, and federal and state judges who participated in the George Mason University Law and Economics Center Colloquium for many helpful comments.

C. Winston (✉)
Economic Studies Program, Brookings Institution, Washington, DC, USA
e-mail: CWINSTON@brookings.edu

© The Author(s), under exclusive license to Springer Nature Switzerland AG 2024
C. Winston (ed.), *Reforming Occupational Licensing in the US*,
https://doi.org/10.1007/978-3-031-74349-8_2

other modes of intellectual thought that could help them improve their policy decisions and rulings when they serve in government as legislators and judges.

Keywords Legal profession · Law school · Bar examination · Law license · Supreme Court

1 Introduction

The Stigler-Peltzman capture theory of regulation (Stigler 1971; Peltzman 1976) explains that certain industries are regulated because regulation seeks to benefit the regulated industry's interests, not to enhance economic efficiency. Peltzman (1989) applied the theory to argue that certain industries were deregulated because it served their interests and indicated that deregulation also would improve economic efficiency (also see, Levine 1989; Noll 1989).

Retrospective evidence showed that deregulating the transportation, communications, energy, and financial industries generally reduced firms' costs and led to lower prices and greater output than prospective predictions of those effects (Winston 1993). Prospective predictions, however, did not account for innovations in industry operations and technology. Those innovations turned out to greatly improve and expand service offerings that raised consumer welfare by as much, if not more, than lower deregulated prices (Winston 1998). The significant changes in the deregulated industries had such an enormous positive impact on American society that Robert E. Litan titled his 2014 book, *Trillion Dollar Economists*, to indicate the credit that economists deserved for their research that contributed to the deregulation movement.

In this chapter, I provide a prospective assessment of an important but overlooked candidate for deregulation, the legal industry, to explore whether its deregulation could result in another economic success story and whether efforts to deregulate it could overcome political opposition. The legal industry, however, has features that distinguish it from other industries that have been deregulated and that do not comport with the conventional Stigler-Peltzman framework. Importantly, the legal industry is self-regulated, and although prices of legal services are unregulated, significant entry regulations exist for firms and individuals that seek to provide legal services and for institutions that seek to educate lawyers.

The American Bar Association (ABA) is the legal industry's primary instrument for self-regulation because it requires would-be lawyers to obtain a J.D. degree by graduating from a three-year law school and it accredits acceptable degree-granting law schools and educational programs. The ABA also has model rules outlining that firms that provide legal services should be owned and managed by lawyers who are licensed to practice law in the United States. Thus, corporations are prevented from competing in the US legal industry and foreign law firms face formidable challenges to establish a notable presence in the US market. Generally, the state legislatures, where lawyers comprise the largest occupational category, have adopted the ABA's model rules and made them state laws.

State legislatures also require would-be lawyers to graduate from an ABA-accredited law school and to pass a bar examination to practice law in their state. Technically, individuals who wish to become lawyers are subject to occupational licensing, which reduces the number of individuals who can provide legal services and discourages those who cannot afford the out-of-pocket and opportunity costs of attending a three-year law school from becoming a lawyer. Individuals who are not licensed to practice law in a state but attempt to do so may be prosecuted by the state for the unauthorized practice of law (UPL).

Another distinguishing feature of the legal industry is that lawyers are the most represented and influential occupation in government. Thus, the legal industry's self-regulation effectively amounts to capturing itself because lawyers' strong influence on all the institutions of government policy maintains the industry's self-regulation and puts the legal industry in a powerful position to affect other policies that may benefit its members at the expense of other members of society. Deregulating the legal industry therefore faces the formidable challenge of overcoming self-capture and possibly reducing the benefits the industry has obtained from its unique position in American society.

I argue that with the assistance of the ABA and the states, the legal profession has operated with self-imposed entry regulations, which have had multiple large, costly effects on social welfare. I further argue that those costs could be substantially reduced by fully deregulating entry into the legal profession. Deregulation would allow the creation of new alternative forms of legal education that would enable prospective practitioners to pursue several viable paths to practice law at a much lower cost than the cost of attending and graduating from an ABA-accredited law school, allow corporations and make it easier for foreign law firms to provide legal services and compete with law firms that currently provide legal services, and eliminate states' occupational licensing requirements and prosecution of UPL.

The market forces that reduce costly inefficiencies and generate significant social benefits parallel those that were unleashed in other deregulated industries. New entry by firms and individuals would reduce the prices of legal services. Such entry also would increase the availability and variety of legal services, which is particularly important because a large fraction of the public, especially individuals with lower income, are not currently served by the legal profession.

New entry and operating freedoms would spur innovation and technological advance by providing the incentive and opportunity for new ideas to take hold among lawyers in private practice that would reduce the cost of and lead to new legal services. Those ideas would come from new legal practitioners and law firms, and from professionals who are trained in non-law disciplines and interact with lawyers intensively in the workplace.

The final and perhaps most important effect of comprehensive entry deregulation is that it would result in lawyers being much less intellectually siloed. Lawyers' broader and more intense exposure to professionals with training in other intellectual disciplines could provide enormous social benefits that other deregulated industries could not provide because such exposure could influence lawyers to improve their policy decisions and rulings when they serve in government as legislators and judges. Expanding lawyers' exposure to other modes of intellectual thought is vital because, as pointed out by Posner (1987), law is *not* a self-contained field of knowledge whose methods of reasoning can by themselves solve human problems in ways that best serve our society.[1]

---

[1] Academic economists and legal scholars do have constructive interactions. For example, Dagan and Kreitner (2021) state that economics has become one of the dominant modes of thinking among scholars about law and policy, and Arlen (2021) points out that empirical analysis of law helps scholars develop models that both predict the effect of legal rules and serve as a foundation for normative policy. Scott and Triantis (2021) argue that lawyers enrich economic models with insights from other disciplines and clarify the connections among those disciplines. One might hope that legal academics would share their insights from interactions with economists when they engage with practicing lawyers. However, Posner (2008) points out that judges, for example, and legal academics, who

2 Entry Barriers to and Deregulation of the Practice of Law

I begin my discussion by elaborating on the three entry barriers to the legal industry to provide greater context for how deregulation would benefit society.

Graduate from an American Bar Association Accredited Law School

Most states require lawyers to graduate from a three-year law school program accredited by the American Bar Association as a condition for taking their bar examination.[2] Most law schools require prospective students to take the Law School Admission Test (LSAT) as part of their application to be admitted to law school.[3] The two requirements immediately discourage people from attending law school who do not score high enough on the LSAT to get into a law school that they believe would enable them to get a good job, and who cannot afford the substantial out of pocket and opportunity cost of three years of law school to become a lawyer.

---

were once close, have grown apart as academic law—influenced in part by social science and economics—has become increasingly critical of the subjectivity involved in judicial decisionmaking.

[2] Certain law schools in Alabama, California, Massachusetts, and Tennessee are accredited by the state not by the ABA, but individuals can, and most do attend ABA accredited law schools in those states. California, Vermont, Virginia, and Washington allow individuals to practice law without going to law school if they pass the state bar examination, and Maine, New York, and Wyoming allow individuals to substitute an apprenticeship for one or two years of law school. Because Maine would like more practicing attorneys to address a lawyer shortage in the state, they are considering a bill that would allow aspiring lawyers to skip law school entirely if they study under a supervising attorney for two years. Kim Kardashian has gained notoriety for her attempt to obtain a license to practice law in California without attending law school. Instead, she is attempting to obtain a license by taking an apprenticeship and passing the First-Year Law Students' Examination and the California state bar examination. Under the Supervised Practice Portfolio Examination in Oregon, law school graduates do not have to pass a bar exam if they instead spend 675 hours working under the supervision of an experienced attorney, create a portfolio of work, and have the work approved by bar officials as an alternative to the traditional bar exam. Finally, Wisconsin allows graduates of the state's two major law schools to practice law without taking a bar exam.

[3] Some law schools have begun to accept the GRE or GMAT as a substitute for the LSAT.

The average cost of a law school education in the United States is currently about $250,000, which is more than three times greater than the cost of a law school education in any other country in the world.[4] US lawyers' annual salaries rank fifth among lawyers from all other countries while, as discussed later, the returns to an investment in a law school education in the United States have become much less attractive since the Great Recession.

The ABA generally does not enable people to reduce the cost of law school by enrolling in a less expensive course of legal education because it does not accredit undergraduate, vocational, online, accelerated, and specialized multidisciplinary law programs. Consequently, those programs are rarely offered to would-be lawyers in the United States.[5] Thus, potential legal service providers are prevented from obtaining specialized low-cost training and using that training to perform useful legal services. Law students also have limited exposure to instructors, fellow students, and eventually colleagues who take different disciplinary approaches to analyzing legal issues. Exposure to alternative approaches and to the accumulated relevant knowledge of different disciplines would enable lawyers to gain new insights that they could apply in private practice and in government service.

Pass a State Bar Examination

States require lawyers to pass their bar examination to practice law in the state, which has turned out to be a formidable entry barrier in practice. For example, Rozema (2023) found that eliminating the bar exam as a

---

[4] https://n26.com/en-eu/the-education-price-index-usd.

[5] Currently, ABA standards state that only law schools with brick-and-mortar campuses can become accredited, and only fully accredited schools can apply to offer a fully online JD program. Jdinteractive, taught by Syracuse University College of Law faculty, is the first ABA-approved online law degree option. St. Mary's University School of Law is the first ABA-approved online-only law degree program. The ABA is currently considering proposed Standards and Rules changes that would enable a fully online law school to be eligible for provisional and full ABA-approval. However, dozens of law school deans have opposed making any changes without more information on the bar pass rates and employment rates of online law school graduates. As of this writing, the ABA has voted to continue examining what standards are necessary to start fully accrediting online-only law schools.

condition for practicing law would increase the US supply of lawyers by 16 percent.

Even when prospective practicing lawyers pass a state bar exam, geographic entry barriers to legal practice continue to reduce the supply of lawyers in a particular jurisdiction and give lawyers and law firms locational advantages in attracting clients. In general, lawyers cannot practice law in a state where they have not passed the bar exam unless that state has reciprocal privileges with the state where a lawyer has passed the bar[6]; they have passed the uniform bar exam (UBE) and their score is sufficiently high that another UBE state accepts it for admission to their bar; or they are practicing federal law and are admitted to appearing in a federal court outside of the state where they passed the bar. Exceptions to the first two entry barriers to practice law exist but only a small minority of lawyers make use of them.

New entry in a state by other law firms does not necessarily result in more competition for legal services that reduces prices. For example, Sidley Austin, a Chicago-based law firm, is planning on developing a presence in Miami, Florida. However, Sidley cannot simply open a new law office and give its employees the option to move to Miami to work on legal issues that arise in Florida unless those employees are licensed to practice in Florida. Sidley is therefore seeking to hire lawyers who are currently licensed to work in Florida and are employed by American Law top 100 firms. Their entry strategy may increase the earnings of lawyers they attract from other firms, but it is unlikely to increase competition that reduces the prices of legal services in Florida.[7]

Geographic entry barriers also can be extended to international markets. For example, a legal case in England involving a New York company could be handled by lawyers who are licensed to practice in New York but may not be able to be handled by lawyers who are licensed to practice in other states.[8]

---

[6] States that offer reciprocal privileges impose burdens on out-of-state lawyers, such as a time-in-practice requirement, different standards for continuing education, and a long wait for approval.

[7] https://www.law.com/americanlawyer/2022/06/02/why-are-chicago-law-firms-competing-in-miami-each-has-a-different-approach/.

[8] The Association of Professional Responsibility Lawyers has advocated a proposal to the American Bar Association, which would change Model Rule 5.5 and allow any lawyer admitted to practice in any United States jurisdiction to practice law and represent willing

Practice Law at Firms Owned and Managed by Lawyers

Finally, ABA regulations allow licensed lawyers to practice law at firms that provide legal services only if the firms are owned and managed by lawyers who are licensed to practice law in the United States. This means that corporations cannot compete in this market and that nonlawyers with expertise in another discipline face an earnings disadvantage when working at a law firm because they generally cannot share in its ownership. Again, lawyers are limited in the intensity of their interactions with professionals trained in other disciplines.[9]

The regulations also may have made it difficult for foreign law firms to establish a meaningful presence in the US market. For example, the "magic circle" of London's top corporate law firms, Freshfields Bruckhaus Deringer, Clifford Chance, Allen Overy, and Linklaters, began to open offices in New York during the 1970s and 1980s. However, they have struggled to make major inroads and are far less profitable than US law firms in the New York market. Some of the London firms are currently trying to overcome US law firms' deep and long relationships with American companies by poaching US trained lawyers with record pay deals and by opening West Coast offices for the first time (Beioley 2022). But they have yet to significantly move the needle while they risk alienating their own lawyers. Finally, in 2023, Allen Overy took the major step of merging with New York's Shearman and Sterling to create one of the largest law firms in the world. Other international law firm mergers are likely to follow. But it remains to be seen whether foreign laws firms' access to the US market by merging with US law firms will increase competition and reduce prices.

In contrast, US based law firms are poaching elite lawyers from "magic circle" law firms and expanding their market share in the United Kingdom. For example, based on UK revenues in 2022, the US law firms Latham and Watkins and Kirkland and Ellis rank fourth and sixth respectively among all law firms that offer legal services in the United Kingdom.[10]

---

clients without regard to geographical location of the lawyer or the client. The proposal, however, has yet to be approved by the ABA.

[9] Washington, DC, permits an Alternative Business Structure with nonlawyer ownership of a law firm.

[10] https://www.ft.com/content/32010275-e063-449e-a52b-0783b826dc23.

It could be argued that market forces rather than regulations explain why foreign law firms have had difficulty establishing a meaningful presence in the US market. However, foreign firms in other industries, such as automobiles and electronics, have enhanced their profitability by manufacturing and servicing their products in the United States. It is not clear why foreign law firms could not succeed in providing legal services in the United States, especially if they involved international legal issues, unless regulations were limiting their operations.

Justification for Entry Barriers

Scholars continue to debate why entry regulations to the practice of law were adopted in the first place given that John Marshall, Abraham Lincoln, Clarence Darrow, and other notable lawyers did not obtain a law degree. Given that efforts to license lawyers began before the Civil War, it is difficult to ignore that racism arguably played a role in trying to limit entry into the legal profession.

Economic theory indicates that occupational licensing of lawyers in the form of a state bar examination may be justified to ensure a minimum quality standard of legal services if consumers cannot distinguish between competent and incompetent lawyers who would take advantage of them. In 1855, Massachusetts became the first state to offer a written bar examination and by 1860, all but two states had established bar exams. However, states did not quickly adopt education standards as a prerequisite for taking a bar exam to improve the quality of legal services for an allegedly uninformed public. Friedman (1962) points out that state legislatures took decades to adopt ABA education requirements because many state legislators themselves were graduates of unaccredited law schools and they would have to admit that they were not qualified to practice law! As more legislators became trained at ABA-accredited law schools, the ABA standards became more widely adopted.

Although occupational licensing may be justified in theory to address an information problem, it is critical for occupational licensing in practice to target the sources of the information problem. That does not appear to be the case in occupational licensing of the legal profession. For example, as discussed later, passing a bar examination is a noisy measure of the quality of a lawyer, and obtaining a law degree does not appear to be particularly helpful in becoming an effective policymaker. Thus, regardless of concerns that consumers can obtain only imperfect information about the quality of practicing lawyers, the fundamental problem with occupational licensing is that it is not targeting the sources of alleged information problems.

In contrast, technological change has enabled consumers to overcome the asymmetric information about lawyers' quality. That is, the proliferation of accurate information sources today about the quality of any service provider strengthens the case that the poorly targeted entry barriers to the practice of law are not necessary to protect consumers from incompetent and dishonest lawyers. The entry barriers, however, are protecting lawyers from greater competition. In the next section, I discuss how the quality of lawyers is affected by entry regulations and how it is likely to be affected by deregulation considering the current and potentially new sources of information on lawyers' performance.

The exclusion of traditional corporations from entering the market for legal services is supposedly justified on the ethical grounds that corporate entities have an incentive to represent their shareholders instead of their clients. However, that justification is lacking because it is not clear why the legal industry is singled out when firms in other industries, for example, health services and entertainment, operate ethically as public corporations.

Deregulation of the legal profession therefore amounts to eliminating the ABA's monopoly control over legal education and mandatory state licensing requirements; allowing any individual to provide legal services regardless of his or her legal credentials; and allowing any firm or corporation, including foreign entities, to provide legal services regardless of whether they are owned by lawyers or nonlawyers and whether they employ US trained licensed lawyers. At various points below, I respond to the arguments commonly made by lawyers that the effects of entry deregulation would not benefit society and would instead harm consumers.

3 Deregulation's Effect on the Prices of Legal Services and on Access to Justice

Economists have documented that entry barriers in the form of occupational licensing have multiple adverse effects. Kleiner and Vorotnikov's (2018) overview of the effects of occupational licensing of many professions in the US economy found that it increases consumer prices and reduces employment. Occupational licensing also exacerbates unemployment by preventing ex-offenders from working in a licensed profession

(Kleiner and Vorotnikov 2018) and by reducing interstate migration (Johnson and Kleiner 2020). Carroll and Gaston (1981) argued that by reducing the quantity of available workers, occupational licensing may reduce the quality of services and consumer safety. For example, they presented evidence that the availability of fewer electricians was associated with more accidental deaths by electric shock from nonindustrial activity. Kleiner and Kudrle (2000) found in the case of dentistry that consumer costs increased in states with more stringent licensing, but that dental health did not improve, and malpractice suits did not decrease.

In the case of the legal profession, Winston et al. (2011) estimated that the various entry regulations have enabled lawyers to earn premiums for their services that were an eye-popping $71,000 per practicing lawyer in 2004, and that those premiums were widely shared among the legal profession based on the distribution of lawyers' earnings and law firm sizes. Given that top partners at some leading law firms serving the private equity sector earn more than $20 million per year, premiums for some lawyers could exceed $1 million per year. And partner pay keeps rising as the average hourly billing rate at the nation's top 200 law firms in 2024 was $1,114, up 36 percent from 2022, and more than 80 percent higher than a decade ago (Miller 2024b). The high prices of legal services, which incorporate earnings premiums, explain why only a small share of Americans ever hire a lawyer.

Instead, many consumers are forced to represent themselves. The National Center for State Courts (2015) found, for example, that 75 percent of civil matters in major urban areas had at least one self-represented party. As more people across the country are foregoing lawyers in state civil courts, judges are reporting that people who represent themselves often do not understand how to formally submit evidence to support their case (Najmabadi 2023). Generally, self-represented litigants face disadvantages because they are less likely to prevail in court and, depending on the size of the lawsuit, it may not even be in their interest to skip work and spend valuable time preparing their case and presenting it in court.

Butler (2021) points out that most people who are prosecuted in criminal matters plead guilty and that the few who go to trial usually lose. Kyle Rittenhouse's $2 million legal defense fund was the rare exception that enabled him to be represented by multiple lawyers, hire a jury consultant, and stage practice jury trials to prepare him for his testimony, all of which undoubtedly helped him to be acquitted for shooting three men and killing two of them during the unrest in 2020 in Kenosha, Wisconsin.

Even when jobs in the public sector are created for lawyers to represent individuals who cannot afford to pay their own legal fees, city offices often find it difficult to attract lawyers for those jobs because the salaries are so low. For example, the median starting salary for a public defender is $63,000 per year, while Louisville, Tulsa, and Oklahoma City pay as low as $45,000 per year. Hourly rates for panel attorneys in New York City, who represent children and indigent adults, have not been raised in nearly two decades and are substantially below the hourly rates paid to panel attorneys in South Dakota, where the cost of living is half of what it is New York City (Bromwich 2022).

As a result, public defenders often have an excessive workload; for example, two Kansas Legal Services lawyers serve nine Kansas counties with a combined population of more than 160,000 people. Given this workload, public defenders are inclined to encourage defendants to make a plea deal instead of going to trial. So-called panel attorneys, independent private attorneys who are offered cases by public defenders, are often unable to help their clients in a timely manner, which forces indigent people to bear the consequences of domestic violence and of children held in foster care. In 2021, half of the attorneys in the Florida public defenders' office who were hired that year decided to leave. In response, the Florida Public Defenders Organization submitted a proposal for final approval by the Florida Supreme Court that would allow law school graduates to appear in court up to one year before they were admitted to the Florida bar.

Effects of Entry Deregulation

Deregulating entry into the legal profession would be expected to reduce the price of legal services to individuals and firms and to increase the supply of lawyers, who would then provide service to a greater share of the public. The following potential sources of new entry could contribute to those effects for different groups of clients. Corporations would enter the industry, and some would provide a variety of legal, financial, accounting, and technology services.[11] Foreign law firms may find it easier to establish a US presence without incurring the expense of poaching lawyers employed at US firms with exorbitant pay packages. Entry by corporations and foreign law firms is likely to affect competition primarily in the higher end of the market by reducing prices and improving and offering new services for industrial and affluent individual clients who currently obtain legal services.

For example, given that New York City is so intertwined with Wall Street, financial corporations that also provide legal services would offer formidable competition to the leading New York law firms by offering lower prices and valuable new services, with some of the cost savings to industrial clients passed on to consumers. Such competition would significantly disturb the "quiet life" of the leading New York City law firms which, based on the number of lawyers they employ, have been the leading firms since 1957 (MacEwen and Stanton 2017). It would be very hard to identify another US industry where the elite pecking order has remained so stable over the course of so many years.[12]

The Big Four accounting firms of Deloitte, Ernst and Young, KPMG, and PricewaterhouseCoopers—among other players—have started to broaden and deepen their relationships with clients who want to solve more business problems in one stop by simultaneously helping them with the legal side of a problem as well as helping them to manage risk, comply with regulations, optimize their supply chain, and implement change management. For example, Deloitte has expanded its legal business service practices by hiring lawyers from leading law firms.

In theory, law firms would respond to the competition by hiring non-lawyers to develop their business consulting practice. In fact, some firms have claimed that they are open to hiring people with backgrounds in other disciplines (Vanderford 2022). However, law firms are currently limited by ABA model rules from doing so because non-lawyers cannot

---

[11] Arizona has taken a recent step to loosen entry restrictions by allowing ElevateNext, a non-lawyer owned legal service provider, to integrate with a law firm to provide legal, technology, and consulting services and by allowing Axiom Global and Counsel to open as a law firm with an alternative business structure, whereby nonlawyers can have an economic interest in a law firm and can offer nonlegal services to complement legal services offered by a law firm.

[12] In recent years, leading Wall Street lawyers' compensation has exceeded Wall Street bankers' compensation. https://www.wsj.com/articles/on-wall-street-lawyers-make-more-than-bankers-now-ae8070a7.

be co-owners of law firms; thus, they have hired only a small number of professionals who are not trained lawyers. Deregulation of the legal profession, however, would enable accounting, business consulting, and law firms to engage in intense free market competition to provide legal and business services, which would benefit firms and individuals.

New entrants who are likely to provide services for less-affluent individuals include people who cannot afford the out-of-pocket costs and opportunity cost of not working for three years to obtain a law degree. Thus, eliminating requirements to attend an ABA-accredited law school would allow legal education to evolve and respond to the diverse interests of potential new legal service providers who could help the public without graduating from a costly ABA-accredited law school. Alternative educational institutions would offer new programs, including but not limited to night-school as well as vocational and online courses of study that could be completed in less than a year at a modest cost and provide certification for specialized practitioners.

In addition, new programs could enable college undergraduates to major in and receive a bachelor's degree in law, an opportunity that universities in foreign countries, such as Canada, the United Kingdom, and France currently offer.[13] Some graduates could immediately provide valuable legal services, such as representing clients in small-claims court, providing advice on simple contracts, which do not require advanced coursework or considerable experience, and assisting indigent people with problems that could lead to abuse or children held in foster care if they are not resolved. The potential demand for low-cost legal services is indicated by the success of LegalZoom, an alternative supplier of basic legal services, which does not require hiring a licensed lawyer.[14]

---

[13] USC Gould School of Law is the first top 20 law school to offer an undergraduate Bachelor of Science degree in legal studies. The University of Virginia Law School announced an initiative to introduce undergraduates to the law school and the legal profession more broadly by enabling them to take a broad range of mini courses from the school's curriculum. In addition, the Law School Admission Council announced a plan to allow prospective law school applicants to take undergraduate courses—possibly in lieu of the Law School Admissions Test.

[14] HelloPrenup provides a digital platform for couples to create prenuptial agreements by filling out in-depth questionnaires and comprehensive financial disclosures instead of having to go to a lawyer. The cost is roughly $600 compared with the average cost of $5000 when an attorney is involved in setting up the prenuptial agreement.

Other graduates could reduce their costs and accumulated debt by completing an accelerated law school program, as occurs in Europe. For example, a combined undergraduate law and J.D. program could be completed in possibly five and certainly in six years, instead of the current seven years. And because deregulation would allow any individual to offer legal services without requiring them to obtain a specific legal education and to pass a state bar examination, some might be self-taught and be able to offer useful services, while others who went to law school but did not pass a bar examination also could offer useful services.[15]

Competition from alternative legal education programs could further expand the provision of low-cost legal services by forcing law schools to reduce their tuition for either in-person students or online courses.[16] Such competition would enable graduates to be less encumbered by debt and increase their likelihoods of pursuing a career in public-interest law or providing more affordable legal services.

---

[15] Examples of individuals who were self-taught and (illegally) provided useful legal services in the current regulated environment include a 15-year-old high school student who became the most requested legal expert on the website AskMeHelpDesk.com and a legal secretary who established a successful business preparing and filing the necessary legal papers for people seeking a divorce (Winston and Karpilow 2016). Harris (2022) describes the case of Marilyn Arons, a nonlawyer, who advised clients in Individuals with Disabilities Education (IDEA) hearings. Arons routinely won cases against school boards, but she was successfully sued by losing schools boards on the grounds that because she was a nonlawyer, she should not be allowed to represent families at IDEA hearings. Finally, Cassens Weiss (2023) describes the case of an attorney who graduated from law school, practiced law for ten years without a license, rising to firm partnership, and eventually passed the bar exam, but was denied admission to the bar after his unlicensed status for several years while he was practicing was discovered.

[16] Online college education has had strong competitive effects on the demand for in-person college education. For example, Deming et al. (2016) found that greater market entry of and enrollment in online institutions reduced enrollment at private nonselective institutions, and increased per-student instructional spending, a broad proxy for quality, at four-year public institutions. Goodman et al. (2017) point out that Georgia Institute of Technology's Online M.S. in Computer Science program costs about $7000 compared with $45,000 out-of-state students pay for the in-person M.S. degree. The quality of the degrees in terms of coursework, faculty providing instruction, and grading standards are comparable, and comparisons of student achievement across the online and in-person formats suggested that the online students finished their courses with at least as much knowledge as their in-person counterparts. It is possible that many law schools would offer both online and in-person law degrees with a much lower cost for the online program, but with comparable quality to the in-person program.

Normally, economists and the public focus on deregulation's benefits from lower prices than on greater output. However, in the case of the legal industry, the benefits from also increasing output or legal services are particularly important because, according to the Legal Services Corporation (2017), some 80 percent of the public are not served by the legal profession. The problem is particularly acute for low-income Americans because 86 percent of their civil legal problems have not been addressed with adequate or professional legal help. Thus, entry deregulation would address the widely acknowledged problem of a lack of access to justice, which has not been solved by pro bono service to the poor that amounts to only 1 to 2 percent of all legal effort and varies greatly throughout the country (Hadfield 2010; Gibney 2019; and Reynolds 2023a).[17] For example, there are 1300 legal aid lawyers in the New York City metropolitan area but only about 1 legal aid lawyer for every 10,000 people living in poverty in Mississippi, Georgia, and Arizona. Nationwide, there are fewer than 3 legal aid lawyers for every 10,000 Americans living in poverty.[18]

In the wake of high-profile violent engagements between police officers and individuals suspected of committing a crime, entry deregulation also may help address concerns about officers' behavior leading up to and during an arrest by improving the legal representation that more defendants receive before and during trial. Police performance could improve if their actions were subjected to more thorough and critical examination by defense lawyers.

Note deregulation would increase competition for and alternatives to incumbent suppliers of legal services and education but it would not prohibit their existence. So, traditional three-year law schools would

---

[17] Policymakers and the legal profession are certainly aware that the United States suffers from a lack of access to justice. The Biden Administration has expressed an interest in expanding individuals' access to legal representation and the courts by providing modest funding for grants to strengthen state and local criminal justice systems, including expenditures on public defenders.
https://www.whitehouse.gov/briefing-room/statements-releases/2021/05/18/fact-sheet-president-biden-to-sign-presidential-memorandum-to-expand-access-to-legal-representation-and-the-courts/.

Some legal scholars and practitioners also are clearly concerned about the problem, as indicated by Judge Richard Posner's abrupt retirement from the bench in 2017 to assist less-affluent people with valid legal claims because he believed that the courts were not treating litigants fairly if they could not afford a lawyer (Liptak 2017).

[18] https://www.abalegalprofile.com/.

continue to exist; the ABA could continue to accredit law schools, as could any other accrediting institution that develops; and people would be free to attend traditional ABA-accredited law schools, take bar examinations, and acquire any other form of certification. If people made those choices, they would become market outcomes that people believed would enhance their legal careers.

To respond to the concern that the marginal educational benefits of a third year of formal law school classes are heavily outweighed by the tuition costs and foregone income, a modification of the traditional three-year law school program also could be offered where law students obtain a law degree after only two years of academic study and pursue an alternative third-year program instead of law school classes (Cunniffe 1997). The third year could be used, for example, to gain experience with a legal externship.

Importantly, entry deregulation is likely to encourage law schools to develop programs that cater more effectively to the diverse career goals of legal professionals. For example, those seeking a specialized education in tort defense, where they primarily defend insurance companies, might take some, but not all, of the required first-year classes and take electives that enrich their knowledge of tort defense. Alternatively, those seeking a rigorous multidisciplinary education, which could prepare them for career paths in academia and government service, could be offered carefully designed programs that include courses in the social sciences, STEM disciplines, and medicine. As I discuss later, this response to deregulation could strengthen the intellectual foundations of lawyers who contribute to the formation of public policy when they serve in government.

Criticisms of Deregulating Entry

A common criticism of deregulating entry into the legal industry is that it is likely to increase the current number of lawyers in the United States, roughly 1.3 million, when it is believed that the United States has too many lawyers. Additional lawyers would include new legal service providers, some of whom do not have a J.D. from an ABA-accredited law school. However, the supply of and demand for lawyers determine the number of lawyers employed and whether the supply of lawyers is excessive. The current high prices for legal services that reduce demand and the barriers to legal practice that constrain supply suggest that 1.3 million US lawyers are too few, not too many, and they help explain why the United

States ranks below other countries in terms of the accessibility and affordability of civil legal services (Hadfield 2010).[19] By decreasing the prices of legal services and increasing the supply of lawyers, albeit increasing the share of new low-cost legal service providers and those wishing to practice public-interest law, deregulation would benefit the public by increasing the number of lawyers who are employed.

A related argument is that many law school graduates never get a job as an attorney. However, this is a choice that some graduates make because after three years of law school, they decide that they are no longer interested in practicing law. This outcome suggests an additional benefit of universities offering an undergraduate degree program in law is that it would give individuals the opportunity to explore whether they should pursue a legal career without making the costly commitment of attending law school and deciding after graduation that they do not want to go into legal practice.

As large law firms raise their entry salaries, currently averaging above $200,000 a year for first-year associates, some law school graduates leave the legal profession because they are unwilling to settle for anything less than a high-paying job at one of those firms. If they cannot get one, they seek to make money outside of the legal profession. This is an example where financial incentives are crowding out any intrinsic motivation for studying law, which deregulation could address by attracting a more diverse set of people who are motivated by more than money to provide legal services.

High-paying law jobs for new law school graduates that provide services to corporate clients would continue to exist in a deregulated legal profession and would attract certain types of graduates. At the same time, deregulation also would lead to a greater share of much lower-paying public interest jobs serving the broader public and would attract many people who are interested in providing those services but who are currently unable to obtain a lower-cost specialized education to do so.

Still another related counterargument is that Winston et al. (2021) find that after the Great Recession, an investment in a law school education may not yield an adequate return for individuals who graduate from

---

[19] According to the World Justice Project, the US ranked 126th out of 139 countries in the category, "People Can Access and Afford Civil Justice."

lower-tier law schools.[20] The problem is that although graduates pay high tuition fees and incur other costs, they generally do not earn high salaries because employers find them less attractive than they find graduates from higher-tier law schools. However, this finding does not imply that there are not enough adequately paying jobs for lawyers per se. Instead, it implies that the high cost of a law school degree, especially from a lower-tier school, limits the jobs that enable those students to earn an adequate return on their investment. Deregulation of the legal profession would address that problem by expanding both jobs and low-cost educational opportunities, thereby producing a much better match between an individual's educational investment and lifetime earnings. In addition, the competition among alternative educational institutions would reduce the cost of traditional law schools, which also may improve the returns from investing in an education from those schools depending on the evolution of the legal job market.

Critics of deregulation also claim that it would significantly reduce the quality of legal services. Paradoxically, this criticism is made in the context of the current regulated environment where considerable evidence exists that entry barriers do little to prevent incompetent lawyering. For instance, Berrey et al. (2012) found that more than half of the plaintiffs in employment discrimination cases thought their lawyers were incompetent. Similarly, Gillers (2014) performed a detailed study of New York lawyers and concluded that the system failed its professed purpose of protecting the public and the administration of justice. Rhode (2004) also argued that the ABA and state bar associations have generally provided weak discipline on lawyers' conduct and the quality of legal services.

Finally, Rozema (2021) finds that after four states abolished the diploma privilege, which enabled lawyers to practice without taking a bar exam if they attended the flagship law school in their states, lawyers who were licensed without a bar passage requirement were publicly sanctioned at similar rates as lawyers who were licensed with a bar passage requirement during the first decade of their careers. Over a longer time horizon, Rozema concludes that bar passage requirements modestly reduced public sanctions. Note, however, in a deregulated environment,

---

[20] Consistent with this finding, Strohl et al. (2024) report that median annual earnings net of debt payments for graduates of law schools whose students' earnings outcomes are the lowest among a ranking of 186 law schools are below $40,000 four years after graduation.

consumers would have more information available that could discourage lawyers from behaving poorly because it could cost them future work and consumers would be inclined to make use of that information when hiring a lawyer to represent them.

Using Hirschman's (1970) framework, consumers do not appear to be effective at influencing lawyers' behavior in the current regulated environment. Hirschman characterized the conceptual ultimatum that confronts consumers when they face the deteriorating quality of goods and services as either exit or voice. In the context of legal services, consumers could exit to express their dissatisfaction with the quality of services provided by withdrawing demand for the lawyer's services. Or consumers could voice their dissatisfaction with the quality of services provided by a lawyer by supplying information about the lawyer's performance that results in disbarment.

However, little evidence exists that consumers frequently respond to a lawyer's poor services through exit or voice. And even when they do, a lawyer may continue to practice and provide poor service for a long period of time. For example, Debra Cassens Weiss reported in the *ABA Journal*, October 27, 2015, that a California lawyer, who was finally suspended but not disbarred, had accumulated more than 1100 pending bar complaints! In addition, lawyers who are disciplined by state disciplinary bodies that enforce rules of conduct reoffend at high rates.[21]

In practice, entry barriers to the legal profession have created only a false sense of security for consumers who assume that ABA regulations and state licensure ensure a certain level of quality that in practice does not always exist. Modern consumer-rights laws, which were enacted after unauthorized-practice of law restrictions, can stop, or at least punish, sellers who abuse consumers.

Economists call legal service a credence good because, like auto repairs and medical procedures, its quality is difficult for consumers to evaluate accurately, even after purchase.[22] Firms and individual suppliers know that developing and maintaining a good reputation for such goods is extremely

---

[21] Rozema (2024) finds that of the 79 percent of lawyers who are not disbarred after a first disciplinary action, 48 percent reoffend and 24 percent are eventually disbarred.

[22] The film *Cape Fear* (originally made in 1962 and remade in 1991) is an example in popular culture of an individual who, after he is released from prison, seeks revenge on the lawyer who represented him because he found out in prison that the lawyer's poor representation resulted in him serving a long prison term.

important if they want to run a successful business. Thanks to advances in information technology, market forces in industries without entry barriers have made great strides to reduce the cost of imperfect information associated with credence goods. Websites, such as Angie's List (now Angi) and Yelp, as well as social media platforms, inform consumers about the quality, reputation, and performance of a broad range of service providers.

Because the legal profession serves such a small share of the public, consumer demand for lawyers is not driven by information on social media. However, websites, such as AVVO and Martindale-Hubbell, currently exist for those consumers who want information about specific lawyers. In a deregulated environment where the legal profession would serve more of the public and information about the quality of a lawyer would become more important, is likely that websites about lawyers would proliferate, offering detailed information about legal service providers for a larger, more discerning, and more heterogenous volume of consumers, who are unlikely to be lured into false assumptions about anyone's competence without supporting evidence. Farranato et al. (2024) study a broad array of licensed professions, which serve much of the public, and find that consumers' demand is more responsive to a professional's reviews than to the professional's platform-verified licensing status.

A facile criticism of deregulating the legal profession is that it is tantamount to advocating physicians should not have to go to a four-year medical school, complete residency training, and obtain a license to practice medicine. The next chapter in this book discusses reforms to occupational licensing in the medical profession. In any case, as noted, many lawyers are likely to graduate from a three-year law school and pass a bar examination or obtain some other form of certification to show they are competent to practice law. Other individuals who wish to provide legal services without graduating from a three-year law school and passing a state bar examination are likely to provide credible evidence that they are competent to perform those services.

Currently, the legal profession does not offer a low-cost alternative to most services, while the medical profession includes nurse practitioners (NPs) and physician assistants (PAs), who have privileges that are complementary to, but not as broad as, fully licensed physicians. Because NPs' and PAs' investment in their education is smaller than the investment that physicians make in theirs, they generally charge less than physicians for comparable services without compromising quality.[23]

Finally, certain critics assert that deregulation is unnecessary because many jobs, such as social workers, advocates, and paralegals, already exist to help alleviate legal problems for less affluent people. However, the ability of nonlawyers to provide much assistance is questionable given that lawyers can run into ethical problems in violation of ABA Model Rules of Professional Conduct if they delegate too much responsibility to nonlawyers. That is, nonlawyer assistants can handle client intake information and answer general questions from prospective clients, but they must direct questions about specific legal services to their supervising lawyer. The limited ability of nonlawyers to provide much assistance also is consistent with our knowledge of the current legal environment, where overwhelming evidence exists that most of the public is not served by the legal profession. It is likely that entry deregulation would lead to a new class of Attorneys' Assistants who, unlike paralegals, can independently provide a range of low-cost legal services.

Recently, the legal profession has shown some interest in trying to lower entry barriers to becoming a lawyer to increase the profession's inclusiveness and diversity and it is debating ways to do so. For example, the Council of the ABA Section of Legal Education and Admissions to the Bar has advanced a proposal to make standardized admissions tests optional at accredited law schools. Historically, the test has been the Law School Admission Test (LSAT), which white test-takers score notably higher on than Black and other minority test-takers do. Affluent students often pay thousands of dollars for LSAT preparation courses that are designed to improve their scores. Critics of the proposal, however, suggest that eliminating an admissions test would place too much reliance on grade-point-averages and other criteria that are infused with their own form of bias.

Certain law schools, including several of the nation's leading law schools, also hope to become more inclusive and diverse by not providing information that is used by the *US News and World Report* to determine its annual law school rankings because the rankings discourage schools

---

[23] https://www.aanp.org/advocacy/advocacy-resource/position-statements/quality-of-nurse-practitioner-practice#:~:text=The%20body%20of%20literature%20supports%20the%20position%20that,conclude%20no%20statistically%20significant%20difference%20across%20outcome%20measures.

from admitting students with low LSAT scores. *US News* will still rank those schools using publicly available information, while other law schools will continue to provide *US News* with information that it uses to determine its rankings. Of course, leading law schools could admit test-takers with lower scores even if they provide information to *US News*.

Proposals to eliminate the LSAT and other admissions tests and to suspend participation in the *US News and World Report* annual rankings are symptoms of not an effective solution to fundamental problems with legal education. The simplest and most effective way to enable the legal profession to become more inclusive and diverse is to allow anyone to become a lawyer without taking a law school admissions test and without graduating from an accredited law school and to allow market forces, not a self-regulated industry, to determine the extent and type of legal education and credentials that are appropriate for a lawyer to perform services demanded by the public.

Clearly, legal service providers who are assisting someone with a basic contract do not need to demonstrate the same level of competence, as indicated by educational degrees and professional accomplishments, as a lawyer representing a client before the Supreme Court or defending the client against a homicide charge. Unfortunately, because only licensed lawyers can practice law, the current legal system forces the public to hire an expensive full-service lawyer instead of hiring a lower-cost effective and possibly superior alternative, who also may increase the profession's diversity.[24]

4 THE EFFECT OF ENTRY DEREGULATION ON LAWYERS IN PRIVATE PRACTICE AND IN GOVERNMENT

Deregulation gave US industries the freedom and incentive to become more innovative. As a result, they improved their operating efficiency and offered new services that provided significant benefits to consumers.

---

[24] Large law firms have been recently forced to kill off diversity recruitment initiatives in the wake of a Supreme Court decision banning affirmative action programs. At the same time, because potential clients may have diversity requirements or might be Black, law firms will have a Black person in their firm attend the client meeting to secure the work. Miller (2024a) reports, however, that those minority attorneys are often used as "window dressing" in the initial client meetings, only to be excluded from subsequent work.

Professionals from a variety of intellectual backgrounds contributed ideas that were the source of new innovations. As the industries adjusted to deregulation and evolved, the following professionals generated and implemented ideas that improved industry performance and consumer welfare.

- Airlines' performance benefited from professionals in operations research to develop yield management systems to set revenue maximizing fares, and from professionals in engineering systems to build computer programs to optimize route networks.
- Trucking's performance benefited from professionals in engineering systems to build computer programs to optimize route networks, and from professionals in inventory/logistics management to determine shipping rates and just-in-time inventory service.
- Railroad's performance benefited from professionals in engineering systems to build computer programs to optimize route networks, and from professionals in marketing and economics to determine and negotiate contract rates and service.
- Financial firms' performance benefited from professionals in marketing and advertising, especially online, to attract and retain customers, and to offer them a wider array of services and products.
- Energy firms' performance benefited from professionals in technology to develop fracking and the extraction of natural gas, and from professionals in hedging and other forms of financial risk management to conduct more sophisticated energy trading.
- Telecommunication's performance benefited from professionals with technical experience to plan network development and to choose among alternative technologies, and from economists to help design the digital economy.

As firms hired more highly educated, skilled, and entrepreneurial workers and used fewer less-skilled workers to perform certain activities, the culture of the deregulated industries focused more on productivity and innovation and less on rules and regulations.

Currently, the legal industry's workforce is generally better educated than the regulated industries' workforce because a law degree is a graduate degree, but lawyers would still benefit from entry deregulation because they would be less siloed and more exposed in law school and on the job to people with different disciplinary backgrounds and experiences who could greatly enrich their approach to private practice and government policy.

It could be argued, however, that such exposure may not be particularly beneficial for two reasons. First, law students already come to law school with different backgrounds, and some have worked in non-law fields before law school. However, most students go to law school to prepare for private practice, fewer plan to work for the government, and even fewer go to law school to become law professors. Even if a law school faculty member takes an interdisciplinary approach to a course, such as a law and economics approach to torts, the vast majority of students are primarily concerned with learning the law, not with how to be an effective practitioner or policymaker. Hopefully, deregulation would change the culture of law school education and experience such that students are more inclined to realize that law is *not* a self-contained field of knowledge (Posner 1987), and that they can be a more effective practitioner or policymaker by appreciating that other disciplinary approaches provide insights on issues that they may think are only legal issues.

Second, lawyers in private practice and government have the opportunity to learn about other fields on the job. For example, antitrust lawyers who work with economists learn through experience how economics can help their case. However, they learn about economics in an adversarial environment where the goal is to win a case for their private client or for the government. This learning environment is unlikely to help lawyers in private practice who could draw on economics to improve the efficiency and productivity of their firm and is unlikely to help government lawyers in a policymaking position who could draw on economics to improve public policy.

Private Practice

Entry deregulation could lead to an influx of professionals with strong backgrounds in management and technology, who could improve private law firms' operations and the quality of legal services.

Management. William Henderson (2017), a well-known expert on US law firms, concludes that law firms' operations are very poorly run when compared with other businesses' operations. Todd Henderson (2017) shed empirical light on the matter by comparing the performance of CEOs with legal training (J.D.s) and CEOs with business training

(MBAs). He argued that the benefit of legal training for a CEO was its focus on the downside of actions, whereas the benefit of business school training for a CEO was its focus on the upside of shareholder value from risk-taking. Henderson found that except for firms that were involved in large amounts of litigation, a CEO's legal training had a negative effect on firm value because the benefits of that training in reducing litigation were offset by the CEO's overly cautious firm policies, which reduced cash flows and growth. Hadfield (2022) argues that the high price of legal services is a consequence of an inefficient business model where lawyers spend a large fraction of their time on office administration and client acquisition, and additional time satisfying licensing and continuing education requirements. Lower-paid workers and new technology could accomplish much of that work.[25]

Because managers of law firms would no longer be required to have a law degree to share in a law firm's profits as an owner, deregulation could result in more law firm managers who have a strong background in management instead of a law degree and who could reduce the inefficiency of the current business model and increase law firms' productivity.[26]

Artificial Intelligence and Technological Advance. AI and other technological advances could have a profound effect on the legal profession. Choi and Schwarcz (2023) conducted an experiment where they gave law school exams to students and found that students at the bottom of the class saw huge performance gains with assistance from the AI program ChatGPT-4, while students at the top of the class saw performance *declines*. The authors conclude that AI may have an equalizing effect on the legal profession by mitigating inequalities between elite and nonelite lawyers.

ChatGPT has not only helped law students, but it also has passed the uniform bar examination on its own by a significant margin, earning scores that approach the 90th percentile of test-takers. Although passing

---

[25] As reported by Smith (2022a), Jennifer Leonard, executive director of the Future of the Profession Initiative at Penn Law, characterized the problem as follows: "If I call up the best heart surgeon in the country and they answer their own phone on the first ring, that would be a cause of concern for me."

[26] Joint law and business degree programs have become increasingly popular, so some law firm managers may have a business degree. Deregulation would lead to more law firm managers having an education and background in management.

the bar does not provide dispositive evidence that a person has an aptitude for legal practice, it is likely that AI programs could significantly contribute to the practice of law and be managed effectively by people with a background in technology. For example, AI programs could greatly improve efficiency in contract review (Martin et al. 2024) and in sorting through electronic discovery documents; improve the quality of legal research and written memorandums; and guide legal strategy by making profiles and predictions about judges and lawyers on the opposing side.[27] At the same time, AI programs such as ChatGPT can cause problems by, for example, inventing legal citations (Verma and Oremus 2023). Still, companies such as McKinsey and Deloitte predict that anywhere from 25 to 40 percent of legal jobs could eventually be automated.[28]

Flood and Robb (2018) argue that law firms have been slow to adopt new technologies because they lack a scientific base from which to analyze how those technologies could improve their operations and the practices of their human capital. In contrast to teaching hospitals in medicine, for example, law has no institutions that are heavily engaged in scientific research and development. It is therefore not surprising that recent surveys have found that 60 percent of lawyers generally (Reynolds 2023b) and 64 percent of in-house lawyers (Guzman 2023) have not used or made plans to use AI tools.

Law firms are not structured to incentivize innovation by attracting strong data scientists and engineers because nonlawyers are second-class citizens at a law firm, and they are typically seen as a cost, not as a source of revenue. Hence, although Reynolds (2023c) reports that AI technology will give rise to a new job title, "legal prompt engineer," with law firms hiring experts to query platforms like ChatGPT to get the best results, many law firms are likely to find it difficult to attract and retain such experts unless they change their workplace culture. Thus, by enabling nonlawyers to share in law firm ownership and corporations to

---

[27] For a discussion of how Major League Baseball gradually embraced new technology, which helped certain teams win the World Series, see Tim Keown, "From Ph.D. to RBIs: How Farhan Zaidi Left Berkeley and Became a Baseball Pioneer," *ESPN*, April 18, 2019.

[28] James Manyika and others, Harnessing Automation for a Future that Works, McKinsey Global Institute, January 12, 2017, www.mckinsey.com/featured-insights/digital-disruption/harnessing-automation-for-a-future-that-works; Caroline Hill, "Deloitte Insight: Over 100,000 Legal Roles to Be Automated," Legal IT Insider, March 16, 2016, www.legaltechnology.com/latest-news/deloitte-insight-100000-legalroles-to-be-automated/.

provide legal services, entry deregulation could usher in a wave of data scientists and engineers who, for example, could implement new technologies and innovative strategies that improve industry productivity and that reduce the cost and expand the range of legal services that lawyers offer to people and firms.

By embracing new technological innovations, the legal profession could potentially improve the public's access to justice. For example, TurnSignl mobile app is designed to give users, who are pulled over by the police, real-time assistance from a trained local lawyer who can help de-escalate the situation while protecting the user's rights and recording a user's interaction with the police.[29] Legal Services Link is an online service that, among other things, connects people needing legal services to address some form of discrimination with lawyers willing to supply that service.[30] Clients post summaries of their legal problem, geographic location, and payment preference. Lawyers then respond, and a potential client compares responses and follows up with a request for more specific information. Given that potential clients tend to be, at best, of modest means and are wary of the sometimes-arduous process of receiving pro bono services, such a service could increase the likelihood that clients will find a lawyer who is willing to take their case (Olson 2016).

Lawyers as Government Policymakers

The potential benefits from entry deregulation of the legal industry may go beyond the benefits that entry deregulation of other industries have provided because they could benefit the broader public by improving public policy. This unique benefit is possible because the legal profession has more influence on government policy than any other profession. More than 100,000 lawyers work in all levels of state and federal government. The profession lays claim to an entire branch of government, the courts, and is heavily over-represented in the ranks of public officials; for example, there are more lawyers than any other occupation in Congress. Since 1789, lawyers also have accounted for nearly 60 percent of the presidents, 70 percent of the vice presidents, and 63 percent of cabinet

---

[29] https://www.turnsignl.com/.
[30] https://www.legalserviceslink.com/how-it-works/attorney/.

members.[31] The prominence of lawyers in government is undoubtedly reflected in the fact that some 20 percent of all law school applicants in 2021 applied to Georgetown University, which in addition to being in Washington, D.C., offers internships with government lawmakers and policymakers.[32]

To be sure, it is more difficult to predict entry deregulation's effect on improving government lawyers' approach to policymaking than it is to predict its effect on the price of legal services, access to justice, and the efficiency of law firms. However, even if entry deregulation modestly improves government lawyers' approach to public policy, total benefits could be large because lawyers strongly influence the laws.

Historically, lawyers have influenced laws in ways that are advantageous to lawyers, but have drawbacks for the public.[33] Consider the following examples:

- Lawyer-legislators are significantly less likely than other legislators to support tort-reform legislation that could reduce expenditures on liability disputes (Matter and Stutzer 2015).
- Lawyer-legislators create tax loopholes that help develop the "income defense industry" for high-net-worth individuals looking to minimize their tax liability (Bonica 2020).
- Lawyer-legislators oppose any effort to reduce anticompetitive barriers to entry to legal practice (Knake 2018).

In addition to the costs of its self-interested behavior, the legal profession's influence on public policy may generate costs more broadly. Considerable empirical evidence documents extensive microeconomic policy failures that have caused American society to incur huge costs (Winston 2021a; Schuck 2014).

---

[31] Congressional Quarterly Press, https://library.cqpress.com/uspoliticalstats.

[32] https://collegegazette.com/georgetown-university-law-center-acceptance-rate-ranking/#:~:text=The%20school%20witnessed%20a%20significant%20spike%20in%20applications,in%20America%2C%202020%25%20%2814%2C052%29%20applied%20to%20Georgetown%20Law.

[33] "Attorney Explains Legal Profession Above the Law on CBS News *60 Minutes* Hidden Camera," YouTube, February 22, 2016, www.youtube.com/watch?v=xY9SC8p4OFA.

Two types of government policy failures exist. First, interventions to address market failures by curtailing the abuse of alleged monopoly power, regulating natural monopoly, reducing imperfect information, curbing negative externalities, and providing public goods have resulted in: (1) significant deadweight losses, (2) missed opportunities to correct market failures efficiently, (3) excessive expenditures of taxpayer funds, and (4) suppressed innovation and technological change.

Second, interventions to address social goals by redistributing income to households who live in poverty, reducing discrimination in various markets, and providing merit goods—that is, goods that individuals or society should have based on some concept of need rather than on an ability and willingness to pay—have resulted in: (1) excessive public expenditures, (2) disincentives for efficient behavior, and (3) unfulfilled social goals.

How are government policy failures linked to the legal profession's influence and how could entry deregulation make the profession's influence more constructive? Lawyers understand and respect the policy-making process and as noted, account for a large share of policymakers. At the same time, lawyers can be overly beholden to their training and professional culture, which may reduce the likelihood of an efficient and effective policy outcome. For example, lawyers in government emphasize procedure and advocacy and the prosecutorial style of congressional hearings instead of a systematic, collaborative search for truth (Miller 1995).

Lawyers also have a predilection for writing laws and regulations and over time have been producing them in huge volumes that run in the thousands of pages. For example, Howard (2023) argues that before the 1960s, thousand-page rulebooks were hard to find. Today, such rulebooks dictating safety are common at workplaces. At the federal level, administrative lawyers are especially comfortable with, and, indeed, may welcome, highly detailed regulations and statutes. For example, the Federal Register exceeds 80,000 pages; the Dodd-Frank Act spawned an additional 14,000 pages on top of its initial 2300 pages; the Affordable Care Act was described in 2700 pages and 1327 waivers; and the Infrastructure Investment and Jobs Act was described in 2700 pages. Nonetheless, such tomes result in ambiguities and a constant stream of legal challenges, instead of initiating clear and effective policies that help to resolve social problems.

Indeed, some lawyers can be so preoccupied with administering regulations that they neglect to consider whether the regulations are enhancing or harming social welfare.

Howard's (2019) critique of the legal profession argues that lawyers share a philosophy of the correctness of the law, such as compliance with a rule, regardless of the law's actual economic and social effects. For example, for more than three years, the Veterans Benefits Administration intentionally stopped redacting names, Social Security numbers, and other personally identifiable information on third-party individuals in claims records provided to veterans. Although people could face substantial harm if their information were misused, the Veterans Affairs' General Counsel's Office simply said there was legal support for not redacting the data (Corrigan 2019).

Lawyers also appear content to determine the "appropriate" legal resolution of an issue without considering its implications, which may motivate a change in the law because the legal resolution is socially undesirable. For example, after Donald Trump announced his candidacy for president in the 2024 election, while facing the possibility of indictment and incarceration for several possible criminal offenses, legal observers pointed out that Trump could serve legally as a US president while in prison without commenting that the constitution could and should be amended to prevent that possibility.

Lawyers' training, career development, and policy perspectives evolve in a profession that itself is shaped by regulations that reduce competition and fail to spur innovation. Such an environment is not conductive to sensitizing lawyers who become policymakers to the vast array of inefficient government policies that also have those effects. In addition, the profession's overly cautious approach to legal education, which has not evolved in decades, and a traditionally risk-averse practice appeals to people who need the security of finding a solution to challenging problems that is undoubtedly correct (Thomson Reuters 2022). Such thinking does not encourage policymakers to acknowledge and correct policy inefficiencies by subjecting previous decisions to rigorous retrospective cost–benefit analyses and by subjecting new decisions to rigorous prospective cost–benefit analyses. Precedent is, well, precedent. Period.[34]

---

[34] Psychologists characterize such thinking as a fixed mindset, instead of a growth mindset.

To be sure, economists have a comparative advantage in performing quantitative retrospective and prospective policy analyses, but an economic analysis must usually go through lawyers if it is to have any influence on policy. Often such work may be ignored or dismissed by lawyers participating in the policy process who believe its message opposes their strongly held views. Schrager (2024) argues that graduates of Yale Law School, who are lawyers not economists, have ascended during 2024 to high levels of economic policy advising on both sides of the political aisle. Those graduates include Republican Vice-Presidential candidate JD Vance and Brian Deese and Mark Pyle, advisors to Democrat Presidential candidate Kamala Harris. During the vice-presidential debate, Vance dismissed economists, including sixteen Nobel Prizewinners who criticized Donald Trump's plan to set universal tariffs on all imports because it would be inflationary and cost consumers, as having PhDs but not having common sense and wisdom.

Schrager (2024) argues that compared with lawyers, economists have serious competitive disadvantages in the political world because they are less wedded to politics and more wedded to economic theory and empirical evidence. Schrager praises lawyers for focusing on big questions that have relevance for policymakers, while economists limit themselves to addressing smaller questions that can be answered using experiments and clever statistical methods. In other words, lawyers eclipse economists when it comes to influencing important policies because they address more relevant questions, but their lack of intellectual rigor raises concerns that their answers are credible and ultimately helpful for improving society.

Consider antitrust policy. Economists disagree on whether enforcement should be limited or strengthened (compare, for example, Baker [2019] with Winston [2021b]). However, my 2021b paper also argues that empirical evidence is simply not available that shows antitrust policy and enforcement have significantly benefited consumers by promoting competition and preventing firms from engaging in anticompetitive behavior.

Obviously, I do not have the last word on the matter and economists generally agree that this debate has a long way to go. Nonetheless, the empirical debate is not even acknowledged by lawyers Tim Wu (2018) and Lina Khan (2017), who forcefully advocate breaking up Big Tech and abandoning the consumer welfare standard in favor of "leveling the playing field" for any and all competitors. Wu and Khan have had considerable influence on the direction of antitrust enforcement because they were appointed by President Biden to the National Economic Council and the Federal Trade Commission, respectively.

Indeed, Khan has stressed her aggressive approach to antitrust enforcement upon arriving at the FTC and has demoralized at least part of the staff (Stacey 2021). Carl Shapiro, the lead economic expert in the FTC's case against Facebook and a supporter of strengthening antitrust enforcement (Shapiro 2019), resigned his position, possibly because his embrace of the consumer welfare standard conflicted with Khan's opposition to it.[35] One might hope that Khan's efforts to level the playing field would promote consumer welfare, but that outcome is certainly not a given.[36] In fact, consistent with lawyers' focus on the correctness of law, Assistant Attorney General Jonathan Kantner has little problem with rejecting the application of a consumer welfare standard because, in his view, it "does not reflect the law passed by Congress and interpreted by the courts."[37]

Economists tend to be more supportive of the efficacy of antitrust policy than they are of many other government policies, in part because economists fill important positions in the antitrust division of the US Department of Justice (DOJ) and the Federal Trade Commission (FTC). For example, DOJ employs more than fifty economists in the Economic Analysis Group that works in the antitrust division, and respected economists from leading US university economics departments have been

---

[35] Christine Wilson, an FTC Commissioner, resigned her position because she believed that as Khan has attempted to remake federal antitrust law, she also has disregarded the rule of law and due process.

[36] The legal industry itself should arguably attract the attention of the antitrust authorities, especially in merger proposals, because of its growing concentration. The top 200 American Law Firms, known as the Am Law 200, account for a large share of total industry revenues. In 2020, the top 50 of those firms accounted for 62 percent of the total revenue in the Am Law 200, which is a substantial increase from their 52 percent share of total revenue in 2000. Given geographical entry barriers in the legal industry, concentration measures overstate the extent of competition that exists because such measures are based on all the law firms in the United States. In any case, I am not aware of any concerns that the antitrust authorities have expressed about competition in the legal industry. In terms of specific activity, the top five law firms accounted for nearly half of the global deal value of mergers and acquisitions in 2021 (Smith 2022b).

[37] https://www.justice.gov/opa/speech/assistant-attorney-general-jonathan-kanter-delivers-remarks-new-york-city-bar-association.

Deputy Assistant Attorney General for Economic Analysis.[38] But it is the lawyers in the DOJ, not the economists, who decide whether to bring an antitrust case, determine the strategy to win it, and provide the remedy if they are victorious (Crandall and Winston 2003).

I am not aware of systematic evidence on the efficacy of government antitrust lawyers to win cases, but circumstantial evidence reported in Winston et al. (2021) raises concerns. For example, until DOJ successfully challenged H&R Block's proposed merger with TaxAct in 2012, it had not won a merger challenge in eight years. Although the FTC has an in-house administrative process in which it rarely loses cases, its own decisions are reversed by federal courts of appeal at a much greater rate than those of generalist district court judges with little or no antitrust experience. Michaels (2022) reports that despite a string of trial losses, DOJ is heading to trial for an unprecedented third time to try to convict executives of chicken processor companies, including Pilgrim's Pride Corporation and Claxton Poultry Farms, of price fixing. Finally, despite the authorities' recent efforts to enforce the antitrust laws more aggressively, the biggest businesses have continued to win merger cases and get bigger.[39]

Such outcomes and the ongoing doubts about the consumer benefits from antitrust enforcement raise a plausible concern about the adverse effects of the premium that lawyers receive from working in the private sector instead of working in government. That is, government's antitrust policy enforcement may be compromised because government does not attract the most able lawyers graduating from the nation's leading law schools. For example, as noted, a first-year associate at a large law firm can currently earn over $200,000 per year and can expect bonuses and significant salary increases. In contrast, a staff attorney at the Federal Trade Commission earns, on average, an annual salary of roughly $70,000 with small raises tied to the federal government pay scale.[40]

---

[38] Economists who have served as a DOJ Deputy Assistant Attorney General for Economic Analysis are listed in: https://www.justice.gov/atr/about-division/economic-analysis-group/past-deputy-assistant-attorneys-general-economic-analysis.

[39] https://www.economist.com/finance-and-economics/2023/09/07/how-chicago-school-economists-reshaped-american-justice.

[40] The National Association of Assistant United States Attorneys (NAAUSA) has drawn attention to another disadvantage facing the federal government in attempting to recruit top legal talent. Currently, lawyers who work in the Justice Department are required to

When the government does attract top lawyers from the private sector for a few years, the effectiveness of those lawyers may be limited by government agencies' resource constraints. For example, Winston et al. (2021) find that, holding observable case characteristics fixed, the same set of top Supreme Court advocate lawyers contribute significantly to winning a case when they are working for the private sector, but they have no effect on winning a case when they are working for the public sector in the US Office of the Solicitor General. The authors suggest two constraints contribute to the advocate lawyers' ineffectiveness in the solicitor general's office. First, the organizational design of the Office limits the time that a top government advocate can spend on a case. Second, the workplace's personnel and environment limit the support that a top advocate can receive.

Accordingly, well-financed people and firms are likely to have an advantage in the quality and efficacy of their legal representation when they oppose the government in a policy dispute because they have the resources to hire leading attorneys who receive considerable support for their work. In fact, companies and private law firms have geared up for the Federal Trade Commission's more aggressive approach to antitrust enforcement by poaching the FTC's best lawyers to strengthen their advantage should they go to court (Stacey 2021). Law firms also have been hiring experienced lawyers from the US Securities and Exchange Commission (Love 2022).

In sum, the documented existence of extensive microeconomic policy inefficiencies, the strong influence of lawyers on government policy, the deficiencies of lawyers in policymaking, and the disadvantages of government lawyers form a credible circumstantial case that improving government lawyers' effects on public policy could produce substantial social benefits. A fundamental source of the problem is that legal education does not stress the importance of retrospective and prospective empirical assessments of public policies, which document persistent inefficiencies in the economy and show how they interact with other inefficiencies. Without this empirical guidance, policy reforms may make things worse instead of better. Of course, society has other goals besides

---

come into work five days a week, while lawyers who work in major law firms are required to come into work three days a week. The NAAUSA is asking the Justice Department to allow federal prosecutors to work from home at least two days a week on a permanent basis.

economic efficiency, but persistent inefficiencies waste resources and make it much more difficult for society to accomplish other goals.

Deregulating Entry to Improve Government Lawyers' Effect on Policy

Entry deregulation of the legal profession could have a positive influence on public policy by enabling lawyers to obtain better preparation in law school for a constructive career in government. Many lawyers in government take a law school degree as a pre-government degree but they do not spend much, if any, time practicing law. For example, Presidents Biden, Obama, and Clinton are lawyers, but they spent little of their careers in legal practice. Law schools could cater to such individuals by offering specialized multidisciplinary courses of study that would greatly improve the training of lawyers who intend to pursue career paths that lead to long- or short-term policymaking positions in government.

Law schools are more likely to design such courses of study if they can focus on their quality instead of on whether the American Bar Association would accredit their programs. Accordingly, eliminating the ABA's monopoly control over legal education is a critical step to giving law schools, including existing law schools and new entrants to legal education, the freedom to think more creatively about developing innovative and useful courses of study for students on different career paths. Indeed, some multidisciplinary programs could be integrated with an undergraduate degree in law, which is currently prohibited by the ABA, so students could take more courses that integrate law with other disciplines instead of taking only law courses.[41]

Examples of potentially useful multidisciplinary programs for lawyers who want to pursue a career path in government include but are not limited to:

- Law, economics, political science, and policy analysis to enable students to gain a deeper understanding of the causes and effects of social science-based public policies. Courses could provide an

---

[41] As noted, students can obtain an undergraduate law degree in Europe. However, if US universities offer such programs, it is important that students also take non-law courses and interdisciplinary courses, such as law and economics, so they are not siloed at an early stage in their legal education, which is then reinforced by a traditional law school education.

empirical overview of the vast evidence on government regulatory agencies' poor performance (Winston 2021a, 2006) and possible explanations for that performance, which may resonate with some students should they work for a government regulatory agency.
- Law, policy analysis, and STEM disciplines to enable students to gain a deeper understanding of science and engineering-based public policies. Courses could provide an empirical overview of government's performance in science and engineering policies and explanations for poor performance, which may be instructive for those students who work for government on science and engineering policy issues.
- Law and medicine to enable students to gain a deeper understanding of health-related public policies. Again, courses could provide an empirical overview of policy performance and explanations for poor performance for students who work for government on health-related policy issues.

A common goal of all the multidisciplinary programs in law schools would be to educate lawyers to be both less dismissive and overly deferential to other, especially quantitative, disciplinary approaches to solving legal problems and to appreciate the strengths and weaknesses of alternative approaches. As multidisciplinary programs evolve, other combinations of disciplines are likely to be used. For example, psychology could be included in certain programs to teach students the role and importance of judgment about policy issues, such as the costs and effectiveness of COVID-19 lockdowns, which reflect judgments about individual and collective psychology.

Generally, the multidisciplinary programs would better prepare lawyers who work in government to broaden their perspective, appreciate rigorous empirically based policy arguments, and work effectively with people who have intellectual backgrounds in other disciplines.[42] Lawyers with such an education who are in policymaking positions are more likely

---

[42] A recent example of interdisciplinary legal education is the Tsai Leadership Program at Yale Law School, which provides students opportunities for courses in accounting, corporate finance, statistics, and more. However, I am not aware of a specialized multidisciplinary law program that has been accredited by the ABA. Villasenor (2022) argues that law professors should co-author academic articles with law students because they are often far better than law school faculty at engaging with information spanning multiple academic disciplines. Formal interdisciplinary legal programs would help students to become better lawyers and research collaborators and would help faculty in their research.

to draw on retrospective and prospective empirical analyses whenever possible to support their policy positions and are less likely to indulge only their ideological preferences.

The idea of improving legal education to help lawyers help our nation to address a fundamental problem is consistent with the objective of a recent open letter from the deans of more than one hundred American law schools, which calls on lawyers to play a greater role in sustaining our constitutional democracy.[43] To this end, the law deans call for the legal training of the next generation of lawyers to include courses that engage with the rule of law and democracy, teach students to disagree respectfully and engage across partisan and ideological divides, and encourage students to support and defend the Constitution and rule of law through clinical work, public education, and advocacy.

In a nutshell, the open letter from the deans wants legal training to help strengthen the nation's political and legal freedoms and to strengthen institutions so they are better able to hold firms and people accountable for when they abuse those freedoms. The goal of the multidisciplinary programs that I outline is for legal training to help strengthen the nation's economic freedoms and to strengthen institutions so they are better able to hold firms and people accountable for when they abuse those freedoms by formulating and implementing more efficient and more equitable public policies.

Another benefit of entry deregulation which has implications for improving public policy, is that it could enable the government to attract more able lawyers by generating more competition among legal service providers, thereby reducing the private sector's relative earnings premium. In addition, greater competition among legal service providers that improves the culture of law firms to make them more efficient and innovative could help government performance if lawyers impart those values when they take leave from the private sector to work in government.

A valid counterargument to my claim that deregulation of the legal profession could have a positive influence on public policy is that most law school graduates who become politicians and policymakers will continue to take the same three years of legal training that current politicians and policymakers have taken. In other words, even if law schools offer multidisciplinary courses for lawyers who want to pursue a career path

---

[43] https://www.americanbar.org/content/dam/aba/administrative/news/2024/deans-letter-061824.pdf.

in government, not many law students will take them. However, the key question is whether law schools would take advantage of a deregulated law school education environment to cater to a more diverse set of students, some of whom would see the advantages in taking multidisciplinary courses to prepare for a career as a government policymaker.

The evidence from previously deregulated industries is that firms have the ability and incentive to attract a more diverse set of consumers than they did under regulation. In a deregulated legal education environment, traditional law schools would compete with new entrants that offer specialized and lower-cost courses of study, which may appeal to some of the students that they normally attract. It is likely that even leading law schools would face more competition for some of their students and would possibly respond by attempting to gain a reputation for providing a high-quality education for certain specific career paths, for example, government service, by offering specialized programs of study. Many law schools may have been discouraged by the ABA's accreditation process from offering such programs in a regulated environment. By attempting to attract students with an interest in government service by developing and promoting a high-quality specialized program, law schools may succeed in improving the education of embryonic policymakers and help to improve actual policies.

As noted, it is more difficult to predict entry deregulation's effect on improving government lawyers' approach to policymaking than it is to predict its effect on the price of legal services, access to justice, and the efficiency of law firms. However, lawyers' outsized role in government—and contribution to government policy inefficiencies—suggest that improvements in both their analytical foundations for policymaking and exposure to people with training in non-law disciplines could change the culture of the legal profession and could result in significant benefits from more efficient and equitable public policies.

Entry deregulation also may help reduce government lawyers' undesirable influence in other settings. For example, the US Department of Defense has more than 10,000 lawyers who insert themselves in every aspect of defense spending. The result is that it takes more time and costs more for project "reviews" than it takes for contractors to complete projects. If new multidisciplinary law programs and greater exposure to people trained in other disciplines improve the culture of lawyers in government, then the public could realize cost savings in many areas of government policy.

5 THE EFFECT OF ENTRY DEREGULATION ON JUDGES

Unlike any other profession, the legal profession lays claim to an entire branch of government, the courts. To the extent that entry deregulation could improve lawyers' performance when they serve in government policy positions by providing them with stronger and broader analytical foundations for decision-making, entry deregulation also could help judges improve their rulings by providing them with stronger and broader analytical foundations. Importantly, those foundations may make it less likely that judges decisions are influenced by their ideological preferences.[44]

Supreme Court Justices' Ideological Behavior

The Supreme Court Justices' ideological behavior has become an important and controversial issue among the public and policymakers in the legislative and executive branches of government because it has a fundamental bearing on the rule of law in the United States. I first present descriptive evidence and observations about the Court's ideological behavior as well as scholarly empirical evidence to strengthen the case that the justices frequently engage in ideological behavior. I then discuss the constructive role of entry deregulation in possibly reducing the likelihood of ideologically based rulings by broadening the Justices' approach to legal decision-making. Such an approach could result in the Justices making regular use of expert panels to provide helpful advice about cases before them.

Devins and Baum (2017) argue that today's Supreme Court is different from past Courts because of the growing polarization among political parties that is shaping the Court along ideological lines. In recent years, justices have been sharply criticized for voting on cases in accordance with

---

[44] It is, of course, difficult to anticipate all the benefits to lawyers, who eventually become judges, from taking a multidisciplinary course of study. For example, Justice Samuel Alito, Jr. defended his action not to report a seat provided to him for no charge on a private airplane flight by claiming it was a seat that would have otherwise been vacant and that his taking it did not impose any extra cost on the private party who paid for it. If Justice Alito had taken a multidisciplinary law program that included economics, he would have realized that there is no such thing as a free lunch or a free private airplane seat. More importantly, an understanding of basic economic concepts may possibly help Justice Alito and other justices in their thinking about cases before them.

their ideologies.[45] Partly for this reason, the court's public standing has sharply fallen. According to Gallop, the share of US adults saying they had a lot of confidence in the court hovered around 50 percent from the 1970s into the 2000s and then began to decline. In 2022, only 25 percent of adults said they had a lot of confidence in the court.[46]

The low point in public approval coincided with the leak during May 2022 of the justices' draft opinion on the abortion case, *Thomas E. Dobbs, State Health Officer of the Mississippi Department of Health, et al., petitioners v. Jackson Women's Health Organization, et al.* When the *Dobbs* decision was officially released with the justices ruling 6 to 3 along ideological lines, it repudiated the 1973 *Roe v. Wade* decision guaranteeing federal constitutional protections of abortion rights, and a subsequent 1992 *Planned Parenthood v. Casey* decision largely maintaining those protections. The *Dobbs* decision confirmed much of the public's view that the justices were making ideologically based decisions. Before the leak, Chemerinsky (2021) raised concerns that the Roberts' Court would have little fidelity to precedent in deciding the *Dobbs* case. In her dissent on *Dobbs*, Justice Sonia Sotomayor argued that fifteen justices since the *Casey* decision have reaffirmed its viability; yet the *Casey* decision was repudiated because the Court has new justices. Sotomayor concluded by asking "If people believe it's all politics, how will we survive?".[47]

The public's confidence in the Supreme Court fell even further in July 2024 when the Court ruled 6 to 3 along ideological lines to grant presidents broad immunity from prosecution for crimes they commit in office, meaning there are virtually no limits on what a president can do

---

[45] Chemerinsky (2014) characterized justices as politicians in fine robes, who simply reflect the views of the president who appointed them. Justice Amy Coney Barrett felt compelled to say that "the court is not comprised of a bunch of partisan hacks" in a college address (Bump 2021). In the aftermath of the rushed confirmation of Justice Barrett, some Democrats raised the possibility that they might attempt to "pack the court" to redress the ideological imbalance, and even introduced legislation to expand the Supreme Court by four justices. Some Democrats pressured Justice Stephen Breyer to retire before the 2022 elections, so President Biden could replace him with another liberal justice while the Democrats control the Senate. Breyer retired before the 2022 elections and gave Biden sufficient time to replace him with Judge Ketanji Brown Jackson, who clerked for Breyer during the Supreme Court's 1999–2000 term.

[46] https://www.voanews.com/a/latest-gallup-poll-public-confidence-in-supreme-court-at-historic-low/6631966.html.

[47] https://www.supremecourt.gov/opinions/21pdf/19-1392_6j37.pdf.

except those limits that are self-imposed by the person occupying the Oval Office. Justice Gorsuch justified the decision as a natural extension of a 1982 precedent that granted former President Richard Nixon and his successors immunity from civil lawsuits for their official actions.[48] However, the Supreme Court avoided the question of criminal immunity for former presidents in that case; thus, Gorsuch's extension of it to justify the court's ruling is questionable. Indeed, President Joe Biden thought the decision was so flawed that he has sought to overrule it by calling for a constitutional amendment called the No One Is Above the Law Amendment, which would clearly state that there is *no* immunity for crimes a former president committed while in office.

Justices have engaged in ideological behavior in specific cases by applying the major questions doctrine or the originalism legal philosophy or following their instincts of what a correction decision should be based on their ideology. Of course, Justices' ideological preferences could coincide with their application of the major questions doctrine or originalism.

Major Questions Doctrine. Vermuele (2022) assesses the Roberts' Court application of the "major questions doctrine" in its June 2022 decision on *West Virginia v. Environmental Protection Agency*. The decision holds that in "extraordinary cases" the court will apply a "different approach" than the ordinary legal principles governing the interpretations of statutes. Instead, the court will demand clear congressional authorization for agency action that is, in the judges' view, "highly consequential," posing questions of "economic and political significance." Vermeule concludes the doctrine amounts to a pretext for the Supreme Court to engage in ideological behavior, which can be translated in practice as libertarian opposition to federal regulation.

Originalism. Attributed to Judge Robert Bork (1971), originalism argues that judges' rulings should adhere strictly to the text and the Framers' original intent when interpreting the Constitution. Originalism currently permeates Supreme Court decisions with Justices Barrett, Kavanaugh, and Gorsuch generally embracing the philosophy and Justices Alito, Roberts, and Thomas often supporting decisions based on it.

---

[48] https://www.msn.com/en-us/news/other/justice-gorsuch-defends-supreme-court-s-trump-immunity-decision-as-he-promotes-his-new-book/ar-AA1olQMj?ocid=BingNewsSerp.

Chemerinsky (2022) argues that originalism facilitates ideological beliefs for several reasons. First, originalism's alleged intent to limit judicial discretion cannot be taken seriously because so-called originalist judges abandon the approach when it conflicts with their preferred outcome. Second, there is no original constitutional meaning to discover in many cases. Third, using an originalist approach in other cases would lead to abhorrent results, such as not providing constitutional protection against race-based and sexual discrimination. Finally, a review of several Supreme Court cases shows that the costs of originalism would have far outweighed the benefits if judges had limited constitutional meaning to that of 1787, 1791 or even 1868, when the 14th amendment was ratified.

Justices' Ideological Instincts. Posner (2008) argued that, because justices do not share a commitment to a logical premise for making decisions (for example, cost–benefit analysis), they must be ideological because they cannot be anything else.[49] This is a powerful indictment to which justices and judges often respond by saying that they simply follow the US Constitution or other appropriate law. For example, Justice Barrett was quoted as saying (Bump 2021), "Sometimes I don't like the results of my decisions, but it's not my job to decide cases based on the outcome I want." Posner has long dismissed that response (see, for example, his 1995 book) by saying that "law" signifies all that is pretentious, uninformed, prejudiced, and spurious in legal tradition. Posner expanded on his perspective in a 2017 interview with Liptak by saying, "A case is just a dispute. The first thing you do is ask yourself—forget about the law—what is a sensible resolution of this dispute?" The next thing you do is to "See if a recent Supreme Court precedent or some other legal obstacle stands in the way of ruling in favor of that sensible resolution. And the answer is that's rarely the case, or when you have a Supreme Court case or something similar, they're often extremely easy to get around."

Justices' ideological instincts are not mitigated in law school because generally they are not exposed to alternative analytical approaches to resolving policy issues or cases before the courts that would reveal decisions that were strongly influenced by judges' ideologies. Their instincts to reject alternative analytical approaches are, if anything, reinforced as

---

[49] The point is not that judges should decide cases based solely on cost–benefit analysis. However, cost–benefit analysis should be a consideration with experts providing guidance on identifying and estimating the costs and benefits, which judges would hopefully consider.

they gain work experience as lawyers and judges in lower courts. For example, when presented with basic statistical evidence of anomalies in the 2019 election of Georgia's lieutenant governor, McDonald (2019) reports that a Georgia Supreme Court justice said: "We are all lawyers. We are all judges. You are making us shudder with math." Another added, "I am one of many people who went to law school because I was told there would be no math. Yet here it is." To take an empirical example of ideology appearing to play an important role among lower court judges, all else equal, Republican-appointed judges in federal district courts gave longer prison sentences to Black defendants than did Democratic-appointed judges (Cohen and Yang 2019).

After advancing to his position as Chief Justice of the U.S. Supreme Court, it is not surprising that John Roberts' response to statistical evidence showing Wisconsin's voting districts had been warped by political gerrymandering was to dismiss it as "sociological gobbledygook," when, in fact, it was a conclusion based on basic mathematical methods (Liptak 2018). If further research corroborates Cohen and Yang's finding about the sentencing bias in federal district courts, would the judiciary investigate the matter or follow Roberts and dismiss the research as "sociological gobbledygook"?[50]

Empirical Evidence of the Supreme Court's Ideological Polarity

Recent empirical evidence shows that justices have made ideologically based rulings that reflect significant polarity on the court. Bonica and Sen (2021) show graphically the growing ideological divide in the Court following the retirement of Justice John Paul Stevens in 2009. Other research has estimated econometrically the effect of justices' ideologies on their votes on cases before the court. For example, Lee Epstein et al. (2013) performed such an analysis based on business cases. Business cases are useful to analyze because justices tend to have well-defined preferences toward business and the policies favored by most business interests, and their political ideology (liberal or conservative) can serve as a good proxy for those preferences, with conservative justices' doctrinal

---

[50] In contrast to Roberts's reaction to empirical evidence, a federal appeals judge, Edith H. Jones, called for a constructive use of social science methodology, cost–benefit analysis, to assess the desirability of suppressing incriminatory statements made to police without a *Miranda* warning.

commitments making it more likely that they will make decisions that favor business firms and liberal justices' doctrinal commitments making it less likely that they will make decisions that favor business firms.[51] Epstein, Landes, and Posner concluded from their estimates of justices' ideology dummy variables that the conservatives on the Roberts court are extremely pro-business and that the liberals are only moderately liberal.

Richard Epstein (2013) challenged their finding on the grounds that the authors did not control for potential selectivity bias in the case petitions that the Roberts court chose to accept. The Supreme Court generally receives thousands of petitions to hear cases every year and agrees to hear only a tiny share of the petitioned cases; the choice of which could bias the justices in particular ideological directions.

Winston et al. (2021) estimated a joint model of justices' votes on business cases and their selection of petitioned cases and found that omitting case petitions does create selectivity bias that strongly affects conclusions about justices' ideological behavior. However, the effect is to mute ideological preferences through the petition-selection process. When Winston, Burk, and Yan controlled for case selection, they found that "liberal" justices have even stronger preferences to vote against businesses and "conservative" justices have even stronger preferences to vote in favor of businesses than Epstein et al. (2013) found. Importantly, the Roberts court has become much more polarized along ideological voting lines than the court under former Chief Justice William Rehnquist.[52]

Although it is difficult to quantify the implications of the Supreme Court's growing ideological polarity for the nation's economic and social welfare, it is hard to imagine that the effects are positive if over time administrations attempt to overturn important decisions made by previous administrations, with the court tending toward extremes that

---

[51] First Amendment, abortion, gun control, and other cases certainly evoke ideological preferences, but their heterogeneity and small sample sizes make it more difficult to use them to estimate justices' ideological preferences.

[52] Ideological polarity also exists at courts below the Supreme Court. Bonica and Sen's (2021) analysis of trends in judicial polarization within the US federal courts shows gaps in the ideology of judges appointed by Republican Presidents versus those appointed by Democrats. Cohen (2023) finds that the ideology of federal circuit court judges, as proxied by the party of the president nominating them, strongly helps to predict case outcomes and that such polarization has grown over time.

are marked by persistent ideological splits.[53] It is indicative that concerns about ideological behavior on the Supreme Court are clearly warranted when Justice Samuel Alito was surreptitiously recorded supporting one of the positions in the current national divide by saying that "one side or the other is going to win" and agreeing that people who believe in God have got to keep fighting to return the United States to a place of godliness.[54]

Entry Deregulation and Expert Panels

Entry deregulation could facilitate changes in legal education and the role of expert panels in legal proceedings that could influence judges to make less ideologically based decisions. Law school students, who eventually become judges, could be exposed to more empirically oriented approaches to legal, or, in general, public policy issues, by learning about and appreciating the approaches to policymaking taken by other more quantitative disciplines. As prospective judges and especially Supreme Court Justices have greater exposure to helpful aids to policymaking, they could become receptive to forming and working with a panel of independent experts from appropriate academic disciplines. Such panels would address Posner's (1987) warning on the shortcomings of relying solely on the law to make policy decisions and, following Posner (2008), would help judges make more pragmatic policy-based decisions by improving their understanding of, and the decisions they make about, cases that involve increasingly complex social and technical issues but may evoke ideological preferences.[55]

---

[53] Re (2023) argues that a judge's personal precedent both does and should play a central role in Supreme Court practice. He concludes that personal precedent is the set of decisional principles—the law—to which a specific judge has publicly subscribed. Thus, justices may appear to be ideological because they do not want to appear to be inconsistent. However, Re does not provide any empirical evidence or a suggestive test that enables one to distinguish between ideology and personal precedent. Importantly, even if they can be distinguished, in practice, personal precedents may have the same effect that ideology has on the court's polarization. In the spirit of Posner (2008), if changing judges (with different personal precedents and ideologies) changes the law, what does that imply about the intellectual foundations of law?

[54] https://www.nytimes.com/2024/06/10/us/politics/supreme-court-alito.html.

[55] President Joe Biden's special commission on the US Supreme Court assessed various proposed reforms but did not consider expert panels.
https://www.whitehouse.gov/wp-content/uploads/2021/12/SCOTUS-Report-Final.pdf.

So-called "virtual briefings" are currently provided online to influence justices and law clerks outside of traditional briefing rules. Legal scholars disagree to some extent on the merits of those briefings, in part because of their lack of transparency (Fisher and Larsen 2019; Baude 2019). In addition, various programs are offered around the country where judges and justices can enroll to learn more about economics, for example, if they have an interest. Ash et al. (2021), conclude that based on the economics language and conclusions of their opinions, US federal judges appear to be influenced by exposure to the Manne Economics Institute intensive economics course, which was popular among both Republican and Democratic appointees. However, the authors do not draw any definitive conclusions about the welfare effects of greater exposure to economics, although they suggest that people who value economic efficiency improvements would conclude that the exposure has socially beneficial effects.[56]

Courts in the United States make use of special masters in some cases, such as disputes between states that are first heard at the Supreme Court level. The special master is assigned to take evidence and make a ruling, which the Supreme Court then assesses.

The expert panels that I recommend are not intended to challenge the court's authority and the rule of law and facilitate judicial overreach. Instead, they would provide an additional and transparent opportunity for justices to benefit from experts in an environment that may facilitate more targeted and balanced discussion. For example, economists could serve on expert panels to provide advice to justices about the efficiency

---

Appelbaum (2022) calls for Biden to put in more judges on the federal bench with liberal views that favor an activist antitrust policy to push back on alleged corporate power that has been favored by conservative judges who were appointed by President Ronald Reagan. Conservative judges have supported more restrained antitrust policy and enforcement. However, Appelbaum's recommendations are likely to be counterproductive for addressing concerns that judges are making ideologically based rulings. An expert panel of antitrust economists, for example, could provide an empirically based explanation of whether a specific antitrust ruling by judges would serve to enhance social welfare and could expose the role of judges' ideological views in supporting a ruling that would harm social welfare.

[56] Thompson et al. (2024) provide experimental evidence that in the face of crowded dockets and time pressures, judges use Wikipedia as a shortcut to stay abreast of the ever-growing body of case law. No evidence was provided about whether Supreme Court justices also use Wikipedia.

and distributional effects of potential rulings. A formal process could be established for long and short-term appointments of panel members.

Objections to Expert Panels

There are several general objections to expert panels and objections specifically to expert panels of economists that I can identify. I summarize those objections in italics and provide counterarguments that, in my view, further strengthen the case for justices' use of expert panels.

The Supreme Court rests its decisions narrowly on the text of the Constitution or, in the case of statutory disputes, is best positioned to resolve them. If this were true, expert panels would not be helpful. However, we know that the Court must decide cases where it has no choice but to balance competing economic interests, such as the merits of antitrust law as applied to a specific industry or contract disputes between private parties. And it often must decide cases where there is true ambiguity about what the government statute means in contemporary context—for example, disputes over the ownership of intellectual property governed by laws written in the nineteenth century. Indeed, if there were no ambiguity as to how constitutional or statutory questions should be resolved, why are not all Court decisions unanimous (when many are not)? Or why don't we have just one justice on the Court and possibly an alternate justice, instead of nine justices?

Expert panels are inconsistent with the role of the Supreme Court. Expert panels arguably miss the point of the Supreme Court's role in the US government. The Supreme Court is supposed to be narrowly constitutional and a check within the structure of governance. However, justices are free to be as narrow or broad as they want in assessing cases brought before them. Posner (2013) argues that justices engage in "motivated thinking" in their interpretation of history to shape how the majority of justices want a case to turn out. Bowie (2021) adds that there is little historical reason to believe there is anything intrinsically correct about the Supreme Court's constitutional interpretations. Accordingly, why not draw on expertise, where appropriate, that could lead to a more informed and socially desirable decision? Finally, Lazarus (2021) argues that advocacy history is increasingly playing a role to help justices evade precedents by considering how parties participating in a precedent-setting case framed and argued it instead of narrowly focusing on the judges' decision and on narrowly constitutional issues. Justices could use the framework of advocacy history to work with expert panels to interpret and apply previous arguments as economic arguments that could shed light on a case.

Economists also are ideological. It can be argued that economists are ideological and their participation in expert panels would introduce another source of ideological bias. However, economists have extensive training that enables them to take a more empirically oriented approach to decision-making than lawyers are inclined or able to take. Importantly, the issues facing the court that involve economists would be appropriately debated over data, theory and empirical methods, and the proper interpretation of up-to-date evidence, thereby leaving little room for sheer ideology. Well-formed expert panels would enable economists to contribute scholarly arguments that are supported by their and others' academic research.

For example, consider the well-known debate about the effects of the minimum wage on employment, earnings, and non-wage benefits, which could be compromised by ideological preferences for or against government intervention to raise the minimum wage. One could argue that among economists an ideological divide exists on the effects of raising the minimum wage that is aligned with economists' political views. However, the scientific debate in the economics profession on the effects of raising the minimum wage continues to evolve on empirical grounds as researchers devise new experiments, data sources, and quantitative techniques to identify the causal effects of minimum wage laws on workers' earnings and benefits. To be sure, the profession has yet to reach a consensus on those causal effects. Nonetheless, this vital field of research illustrates how economists who are actively engaged in a research program can draw on a sophisticated body of empirical evidence to shed scientific light on issues before the Supreme Court even if those issues provoke ideological responses among some justices and economists.[57]

An expert panel of economists should not be expected to always reach a consensus about what the evidence that they are considering suggests about the economic effects of a ruling in a particular case. However, a

---

[57] Recent papers assessing the effects of the minimum wage appear on a regular basis, such as Esposito et al. (2021) and Karabarbounis et al. (2022). New papers assessing the minimum wage that will be published in 2024 include an exchange between Dube and Jha, Neumark, and Rodriquez-Lopez.

balanced discussion of the relevant analytical issues and empirical findings would still be informative to justices in their deliberations.

Economist and non-economist experts may disagree. Because justices should form expert panels consisting of economists and of experts in other fields, there may be cases where economists and non-economists reach different conclusions about the evidence. In my view, these are the type of cases where participants in expert panels should rigorously debate their views and justices should attempt to make constructive use of those views.

For example, in the run-up to the Supreme Court's decision on the *Dobbs v. Jackson Women's Health Organization* abortion case, opposing briefs were filed on the economic effects of abortion. One *amicus curiae* brief filed by more than 150 economists argued that "abortion significantly impacts women's wages and educational attainment, with impacts most strongly felt by black women."[58]

Two briefs were filed that disagree with economists on the importance of *Roe v. Wade* in advancing women's quality of life over the past several decades. The main brief filed by the petitioners opposed abortion rights but did not include separate views discussed by experts.[59] The second brief was a friend of the court brief filed by 240 signers who are female scholars and professionals mainly with law or medical degrees; only a handful had an economics doctoral degree.[60] That brief indicates that the evidence suggests *Roe* did not help women economically and, in fact, may have been harmful. In addition, Catherine Pakaluk,

[58] https://reproductiverights.org/wp-content/uploads/2021/09/Economists-Amicus-Brief.pdf. Knowles Myers and Welch (2021) summarize research on the effect of abortion access on women's lives. Miller et al. (2023) recently linked credit report data to the Turnaway Study, which collected high-quality, longitudinal data on women receiving or being denied a wanted abortion in the United States, and found that women who were denied an abortion experience a large increase in financial distress that remains for several years.

[59] https://www.supremecourt.gov/docketpdf/19/19-1392/184703/20210722161332385_19-1392briefforpetitioners.pdf?campaign_id=228&emc=edit_pc_20220520&instance_id=61918&nl=petercoy&regi_id=66103189&segment_id=92877&te=1&user_id=dfba3090c5cf32a59661f3880a68ad97.

[60] https://www.supremecourt.gov/docketpdf/19/19-1392/185586/2021080311413494_19-1392%20brief%20of%20240%20women%20scholars%20et%20al%20in%20support%20of%20petitioners%20replacement%20copies.pdf?campaign_id=228&emc=edit_pc_20220520&instance_id=61918&nl=petercoy&regi_id=66103189&segment_id=92877&te=1&user_id=dfba3090c5cf32a59661f3880a68ad97.

an economics professor at Catholic University, argues that a complete cost–benefit assessment should account for the effects of abortion on the unborn child.

Given the disagreement, it would have been valuable for the justices before they made their decision on the *Dobbs* petition to hear from experts in separate panels and to bring the experts together in a final panel that attempted to reconcile opposing views and the implications of the evidence. To be sure, the experts may have remained split on the evidence; however, holding a formal discussion, debate, and analysis of opposing views would be a significant improvement over much current practice where judges and justices conclude from conflicting testimony about empirical evidence that experts simply disagree without attempting to have a focused discussion that may clarify and even resolve areas of disagreement.

Experts can submit amicus curiae briefs. As discussed, experts can submit *amicus curiae* briefs if they wish to have some effect on Supreme Court decisions. However, it is not clear that such briefs have much impact if judges do have attempt to reconcile conflicting views. In addition, *amicus curiae* briefs are likely to have little impact if they are not invited. When Richard Posner was serving as a judge on the Seventh Circuit, he claimed that the amicus briefs filed in his court provided little or no assistance to judges because they largely duplicated the positions and arguments of the parties (Kearney and Merrill 2000, p. 245). To the extent that briefs appear to have any impact, they are more concerned with legal matters not with broader policy issues, which would be the focus of expert panels.

The Supreme Court makes legal not economic decisions. One could question why exposure to critical information would help to reduce the influence of ideology on justices' decisions, especially if the Supreme Court, in theory and in practice, makes legal decisions not economic decisions. Ash et al. (2021) point out that in a common-law system, judges have significant discretion in their decisions. If, for example, judges take economic ideas to heart, they may reach very different decisions, despite working within shared legal rules. This discretionary aspect of judging leaves scope for ideas, such as economics, to have a constructive influence on judges' decision-making process. Indeed, it is fair to characterize Posner's approach as using economic analysis to decide a particular case and then finding a legal argument to justify the decision. I have stressed that by increasing lawyers' exposure to the strengths of other disciplines besides law, deregulation could have a constructive effect when those lawyers are in policymaking positions in legislatures or as judges.[61]

Further, even if one contends that the Supreme Court does not make ideological decisions, Katz (2021) argues that they do incorporate economics in their decisions. Katz further argues that the courts often base their antitrust decisions, for example, on unfounded empirical claims or the misapplication and misinterpretation of economics. Entry deregulation that helps to improve lawyers' and subsequently judges' exposure to economics to the point where they recognize their limitations to understanding a sophisticated economic analysis would have a constructive effect by helping judges to be more inclined to form an expert panel of economists to reduce the likelihood that their decision is criticized for misunderstanding and misusing economics.

The legislative branch should convene expert panels. Notwithstanding the constructive purpose of expert panels, the legislative branch is supposed to draw upon experts and look at the big picture. Bowie's (2021) response is that the Supreme Court arbitrarily dominates Congress: even when the court is permissive, Congress can make no law without its permission. Thus, the Supreme Court does consider the big picture and given that the legislative branch has become fractured and has not been objectively debating policies for decades, it is even more important for the judicial branch to continue to do so and increase its engagement with experts. At the very least, it would be useful for justices to know whether specific legal arguments and rulings were inconsistent with promoting economic efficiency or progressive redistribution goals. As noted, the law is generally

---

[61] Lawyers frequently use a variant of Posner's approach—decide on the desired outcome and find the legal argument to support it—but this can create significant costs when lawyers are in policymaking positions and other relevant issues are not considered. Consider the recent effort by the Biden Administration, which wanted to protect renters from being evicted, when they were confronted with the problem that a national eviction moratorium could not be extended. President Biden told Chief of Staff Ron Klain to ask Professor Laurence Tribe of Harvard to devise an alternative legal argument to maintain the eviction moratorium. Tribe's solution was to impose a new and different moratorium with effectively the same outcome, rather than try to extend the original moratorium. The Supreme Court recently blocked Biden's moratorium, writing that "if a federally imposed eviction moratorium is to continue, Congress must specifically authorize it." The Posnerian approach, which I support, would determine the optimal long-run economic approach to evictions, accounting for all the relevant costs and benefits, and find the law to support it.

not so narrow that it prevents rulings that could be more aligned with economic objectives.

Lawyers control the evidentiary process. Lawyers insist on controlling the evidentiary process, so it would be difficult to integrate expert panels into the adversarial, lawyer-dominated system of witness selection, examination, and compensation. However, the Supreme Court solicits *amicus curiae* briefs, for example, from the Solicitor General's Office, for insights into the legal issues involved in a case (Winston et al. 2021). The Supreme Court's formation of expert panels would serve to gain insights into economic and other issues that are relevant for deciding a case.

Expert panels would amount to academic seminars. Expert panels may appear to be too academic and could turn court deliberations into seminars with no practical insights that improve decisions. Historically, justices and academics were close. Bazelon (2015) describes how Justice Oliver Wendell Holmes Jr. was influenced by a Harvard instructor, Harold Laski, to read John Stuart Mill and Adam Smith, and how those works caused him to change his views on the freedom of speech. Brazen notes judges rarely change their minds today because they wrap themselves in a mythos of authority and certainty. The goal of expert panels would be to enable justices and academics to bridge their distance and have a closer and more constructive intellectual relationship.

In addition, expert panels should not be restricted to academics. Economists and people from all walks of life should be recruited to help analyze a case if they have credible expertise to draw on empirical, institutional, and experience-related evidence as appropriate. Ultimately, the justices would determine the effectiveness of expert panels. However, the panels would be more effective if justices were no longer siloed in their intellectual development as lawyers and if they were able to appreciate the insights that people from other disciplines can bring to help decide a case.

Other reforms are available. There are other reforms besides expert panels that may improve the Supreme Court, including term limits, age limits, lottery selection of justices, and explicit partisan balance requirements for court membership. In fact, President Joe Biden recently announced his support to create a system in which the president would appoint a justice every two years to spend a maximum of 18 years in active service on the Supreme Court.

Hemel (2021), however, argues that those proposals are unlikely to be effective and proposes instead that presidents be limited to two-lifetime appointments per presidential term and that the size of the court be allowed to fluctuate within bounds. Neither of Hemel's proposals necessarily conflict with the expert panels that I recommend.

Finally, as part of law schools' evolution to a more multidisciplinary educational program, it may be useful for Supreme Court clinics that exist at the top-tier law schools and that are run by professors who are experienced Supreme Court advocates, to experiment with expert panels in their deliberations. Law schools have the advantage that they can draw on their university's faculty in other departments and possibly on other universities' faculty to comprise expert panels. The Supreme Court, which has recently been persuaded by a law school Supreme Court clinic to grant cert to a petition, may find that the clinics' experience with expert panels is informative about their potential utility.

6 Summary and Potential Sources of Momentum for Regulatory Reform

The legal industry does not fit the standard profile of a regulated industry. At the same time, the effects of its regulation may be generating larger and more extensive costs than have regulations of other US industries. First, the legal industry regulates itself with entry regulations that prevent people, firms, and educational institutions from providing competition that could raise social welfare. Second, the strong presence of lawyers in government results in the legal profession being self-captured, which enables it to maintain its entry barriers and to be in a powerful position to influence other public policies that benefit its industry.

The combined costs of self-regulation and self-capture suggest that deregulating the legal industry could potentially have much greater effects on American society than deregulating other US industries. Lawyers are involved in virtually every aspect of human beings' cooperation with each other to accomplish personal and social goals. By making pricing, production, and the availability of legal services more efficient, deregulation of the legal industry would improve cooperation within firms, between firms and consumers, and among people. And by greatly increasing lawyers' exposure to professionals with different disciplinary backgrounds and approaches to solving policy problems, deregulation would enable democratic government to become more effective.

In practice, deregulating the legal industry would incorporate three important policy changes, each of which could lead to significant changes affecting the legal profession and legal services.

- First, educational or licensing requirements for any individual to provide legal services in the United States would be eliminated. This could lead to undergraduate law degrees, and vocational, online, accelerated, and specialized multidisciplinary law programs. Conventional law schools could change their curricula without being concerned about the ABA's reaction and offer, for example, required courses in empirical methods, cost–benefit analysis, and policy evaluation. The increased supply of legal service providers could lead to greater access to justice. Finally, improvements in education and more exposure to other disciplines could improve private legal practice and public policy, and reduce ideological-based rulings, especially if judges and justices make constructive use of expert panels.
- Second, restrictions that prevent or limit corporations and foreign law firms from providing legal services in the United States would be eliminated. This change would increase competition in domestic and international legal services, which would reduce legal fees and result in additional legal services, some of which could be part of a comprehensive package of business services.
- Third, geographical entry barriers that prevent or limit people and law firms from providing legal services in any part of the United States would be eliminated. This change would facilitate greater domestic competition for legal services, which again would reduce legal fees and result in additional legal services, some of which could be part of a comprehensive package of business services.

As in other industries that were deregulated, deregulating the legal industry would require a significant and, for some, a very difficult adjustment. State licensing requirements and ABA accreditation policies and regulations are a form of cooperation that currently substitutes a self-interested association's judgments, which are aided and abetted by government, for the judgments of people and firms. In contrast, I have argued that free markets in a deregulated legal industry would be a superior form of cooperation where self-interested people and firms would make their own judgments and choices in a more competitive environment. Aspiring legal service providers would have a broader choice of education and career choices; firms would have a broader choice of services to provide and markets to serve; and consumers would have broader choices of legal service providers to hire and information sources to consult.

Wrong choices would undoubtedly occur and lead to mistakes. Some people who could not have practiced law under the current regime because they could not obtain a license will turn out to be incompetent and provide poor service; some online and vocational courses will not prepare people to provide useful legal services; some corporations and foreign law firms will behave unethically; many traditional law firms may fail because they are unable to adjust to the new competitive environment; and some consumers will hire incompetent legal service providers. Those possible outcomes would not be surprising because all US industries that were deregulated experienced variants of them as they undertook the long adjustment process to deregulated competition. However, the industries, consumers, and the nation overall benefited by going through the difficult adjustment to deregulation.

Peltzman (1989) argued that the capture theory of regulation could explain deregulation to the extent that certain regulated industries were deregulated because they eventually concluded that regulation was creating more costs than benefits to them, and that they would be better off if the government deregulated them by abolishing the regulations that governed their operations and the regulatory agencies that implemented them. It is therefore somewhat encouraging that aspects of complete deregulation that I have called for, including allowing undergraduates to take law courses and nonlawyers to provide certain legal assistance, are being explored. It also is encouraging that legal scholars—and even practitioners—have identified some of the same problems with the legal profession that I have identified here and have expressed support for a subset of the deregulatory actions that I have recommended.[62] Nonetheless, it is doubtful that the legal profession would eventually conclude independently that it would be better off if it took sweeping actions to completely deregulate itself, so the possibility of deregulation occurring

---

[62] For example, Justice Gorsuch and Nitze (2024) discuss the crisis in the public's access to justice and the efforts by the legal profession to impede the entry of low-cost legal service providers, such as LegalZoom; Howarth (2022) argues that licensing rituals for lawyers protect members of the profession from new entrants more than they protect the public from incompetent lawyering; and Knake (2018) and Barton and Bibas (2017) argue that the ABA's monopolization over education and legal practice should be reformed to allow additional practitioners to provide legal services, thereby increasing the public's access to justice.

depends on external regulatory or legal actions or some type of economic or technological shock.

Potential Sources of Momentum for Regulatory Reform

It is indeed possible that regulatory actions taken by the states, legal actions taken by private litigants, and a technological shock caused by artificial intelligence could provide sufficient momentum that leads to regulatory reform that eventually culminates in deregulation.

Regulatory reform initiated by the states. Some states have begun to form task forces to consider, and a few are experimenting with, loosening restrictions on nonlawyers providing service, which may result in one state "going big" and significantly loosening ABA regulations and licensing requirements.[63] Of course, such experiments will require political support. The Delaware Supreme Court, for example, announced that in March 2022 the state would start allowing nonlawyers to represent tenants in eviction cases. Support from state supreme court judges is likely to be a major factor in helping other states to move forward with a similar experiment.

---

[63] Packel (2021) and Ward (2022) provide summaries of the states experimenting with regulatory reforms and the states that are planning to do so. Engstrom et al. (2022) suggest there are reasons to be encouraged by the reforms that are addressing the justice gap by relaxing rules on nonlawyer participation in the legal system. Specifically, they find that the Utah model—which allows entities to seek waivers of the state's unauthorized practice of law rules— was effective at helping lower-income and indigent people with their legal problems, while the Arizona model—which permits nonlawyers to take an ownership interest in law firms without reforming its UPL laws—was successful at serving a middle-income and small business clientele. Data and information reported by Utah and Arizona regulators indicate that the authorized entities do not draw a higher number of consumer complaints when compared with their lawyer counterparts. The Washington Supreme Court has approved an alternative to passing a bar exam to obtain a license to practice law where law students would be allowed to complete twelve qualifying skills credits and work as a licensed intern They would then be required to submit a portfolio of this work to waive the bar exam. Arizona's Supreme Court ordered the launch of the Arizona Lawyer Apprentice Program as a way to boost the number of lawyers "serving the public in rural Arizona and in public law firms." Arizona is 49th of 50 states in lawyers per capita. Under the program, test takers who come within ten points of passing the Arizona bar exam score can earn licensure after completing a two-year apprenticeship program in an underserved area. Finally, Colorado, Minnesota, New Hampshire, and Oregon also have licensing programs for paraprofessionals so they can perform limited legal work, and the Texas Access to Justice Commission is supporting such a program.

A promising example emerged when the California Paraprofessional Program Working Group proposed various recommendations in 2021, including the approval for licensed paraprofessionals to provide legal services in several practice areas, such as family law, consumer debt, and housing eviction, and to own a minority interest in law firms. However, 90 percent of the commenters on the proposal who were known to be attorneys opposed the recommendations, while 75 percent of those known to be non-attorneys supported the recommendations.[64] The recommendations were then revised to exclude certain areas from paraprofessional practice and to prevent paraprofessionals from owning a minority interest in law firms. Unfortunately, in the summer of 2022, the California Legislature—acting at the urging of trial lawyers who wanted to stifle competition—passed a bill preventing the State Bar of California from continuing its working groups studying regulatory reform. Those groups could have eventually recommended reforms that set the standard for the rest of the country by prioritizing consumers' welfare over lawyers' welfare. In any case, other states will be considering reforms in the future and may implement them.

Assuming a state overcomes political opposition to deregulatory experiments—an admittedly strong assumption—and that those experiments show that reforms have reduced prices for and increased access to legal services, other states could be motivated to perform similar experiments. There is precedent for this path to greater reliance on market forces. For example, California's and Texas's successful airline deregulation experiments provided critical evidence that eventually led to airline deregulation nationwide (Levine 1965).[65] Education Savings Accounts, which households can use to opt out of the public school system and get several thousand dollars in an account that they can use for private school tuition, homeschooling, or other education expenses, did not attract national interest until West Virginia enacted its program, known as the Hope

---

[64] https://www.abajournal.com/news/article/revised-proposal-to-license-nonlawyer-paraprofessionals-in-california-nixes-jointly-owned-law-firms/.

[65] Ironically, Michael Levine, a lawyer, showed in a 1965 law review article that unregulated intrastate round-trip fares from Los Angeles to San Francisco were considerably lower than round-trip fares regulated by the Civil Aeronautics Board on an interstate route of comparable distance, Washington, DC, to Boston. Then Law Professor Stephen Breyer relied on Levine's evidence for the 1975 hearings on airline deregulation that he organized for Senator Edward Kennedy and that eventually led to the 1978 Airline Deregulation Act.

Scholarship Program, in 2021. Several states are now considering similar programs and some, such as Arizona's, are moving forward.

Litigation and regulatory reform. It also is possible that litigation may lead to regulatory reform by eventually succeeding in challenging the constitutionality of the unauthorized practice of law (UPL) restrictions. Justice Neil Gorsuch (2019) raises this possibility on First Amendment grounds, and Cotton (2017) provides support by arguing that nonlawyers' legal advice is speech protected by the First Amendment and that UPL restrictions that exist in most states violate the First Amendment.[66]

Upsolve recently tested this argument by filing a First Amendment challenge against the New York State Attorney General's Office for unconstitutional policies that prevent low-income New Yorkers from getting free legal advice from nonlawyers in consumer debt suits. The United States District Court for the Southern District of New York upheld Upsolve's challenge by ruling that UPL rules cannot be applied to Upsolve's program because the "First Amendment protects their legal advice as speech, and the UPL rules are not narrowly tailored to satisfy strict scrutiny in this context."[67]

Regulatory reform spurred by a technological shock. Finally, a technological shock, such as artificial intelligence (AI), has the potential to increase lawyers' productivity and reduce costs in the legal profession. AI also could help lawyers provide new services by significantly reducing the time and personnel it takes to obtain information to answer legal questions.

Importantly, AI could enable nonlawyers to replace lawyers for many tasks, especially those that nonlawyers can accomplish using ChatGPT. However, this change could raise questions whether its users are guilty of UPL violations. Simon et al. (2018) discuss the case of *Lola v. Skadden*, in which the Second Circuit stated that "tasks that could otherwise be performed entirely by a machine" could not be said to fall under the

---

[66] Recent litigation struck a blow against state bar associations. A federal appeals court ruled that the mandatory state bar in Texas violates lawyers' First Amendment rights because of its political and ideological activities and that the plaintiffs cannot be compelled to be members of the State Bar of Texas pending resolution of the remedies phase. The case reached the US Supreme Court along with two petitions on the matter from Michigan and Oklahoma, but the Court denied all the petitions.

[67] https://uploadsssl.webflow.com/60d147561d53665ec78fff2c/628d5e88d906590 d89beece2_2022-05-24%20Opinion%20%5Bdckt%2068_0%5D.pdf.

"practice of law." Accordingly, the court distinguished between mechanistic tasks and legal tasks and opened a new source of entry that would not be subject to UPL statutes. Machines could evolve and eventually encroach on the practice of law, but their tasks would not, at this point, be regulated by professional rules governing the legal profession.[68]

Indeed, as in the case of other industries, technological change could lead to deregulation of the legal industry as lawyers engage in evolving technology competition, which enable lawyers and law-firms that effectively adopt AI to reduce costs and expand their services. The importance of adopting AI successfully will motivate lawyers to work closely together with data scientists to realize AI's full capabilities and to verify its performance and reduce potential harms from security threats and privacy shortfalls (Leong and Hall 2021).

At the same time, legal education would have to accommodate a more diverse set of practitioners, such as AI specialists, who wish to attend law school to enhance their effectiveness in the legal industry but who do not want to take only law classes for three years. Integrating professionals with an AI background into the legal profession could then provide a template for integrating professionals with other intellectual backgrounds into the profession, which could provide sufficient incentives for the legal industry to support reforms that may eventually lead to it deregulating itself.

Final Comments

Kronman (1993) lamented the decline of lawyers as public-spirited statesmen who have practical wisdom. He argued that many lawyers have lost their ideals and their motivation for a career in law, which is an ominous sign. In recent years, the legal profession's lack of public spiritedness has manifested itself in:

- Practitioners who have been willing to bring dozens of weak cases to overturn the 2020 presidential election and go to any lengths to delay the federal criminal trials of former President Donald Trump, so he could prevent those cases from moving forward if he were elected to a second presidential term.

---

[68] DoNotPay calls itself a robot lawyer because it uses artificial intelligence. It provides legal services through online subscriptions. It does not have a license to practice law, but it has not yet been found to be guilty of UPL.

- Judges who are increasingly making ideologically based decisions and whose questionable ethical behavior has caused President Joe Biden to call for the establishment of a binding code of conduct for the Supreme Court.
- And policymakers who are doing little to enable the vast majority of the public to obtain legal services at a cost they can afford.

Accordingly, my call for the legal profession to be deregulated can be interpreted as a call for market forces to encourage the legal profession to become more public spirited.[69]

The traditional route to deregulation is that policymakers, including but not limited to those trained as lawyers, would be supportive of deregulating the legal industry and would try to sell the public on the idea. However, this approach is unlikely to be followed because, in contrast to other industries that were eventually deregulated and despite the costly inefficiencies that I have discussed here, the legal industry's performance does not appear to most of the public and to academic and policymaking communities to be sufficiently poor to justify sweeping regulatory reform. The (high) prices of legal services do not attract broad attention or cause much uproar, limited access to justice is accepted by most people, operating inefficiencies are not widely acknowledged, lawyers per se are not singled out as a major cause of inefficient government policy, and partisan judges are not associated with the profession's self-regulation.

At the same time, based on the prospective evidence on the likely effects of deregulating the legal industry presented here, it is likely that many members of the public, policymakers, and public-spirited members of the legal industry would find it credible that social welfare could significantly improve if they compared the counterfactual of legal industry deregulation with continued self-regulation. While there has been limited interest by the states and private litigants in piecemeal explorations of

---

[69] In an address to a House of Delegates, ABA President-elect Michelle Behnke spoke about the importance of lawyers in combating tyranny. However, she did not comment on how lawyers can be used to facilitate tyranny and on what could be done to prevent lawyers from playing that role.
https://www.abajournal.com/web/article/lawyers-essential-to-fighting-tyranny-says-aba-president-elect-michelle-behnke?utm_source=sfmc&utm_medium=email&utm_campaign=weekly_email&promo=&utm_id=880182&sfmc_id=50745240.

whether this outcome would occur in practice, the more promising possibility exists that the legal industry could be convinced by a technological shock that it would be in its interest to be deregulated. If that occurs, the legal industry will succeed in getting the regulatory reform it wants and that everyone else should want.

REFERENCES

Appelbaum, Binyamin. 2022. When Picking Judges, Democrats Need to Stop Ignoring Economics. *New York Times*, June 1.

Arlen, Jennifer. 2021. The Essential Role of Empirical Analysis in Developing Law and Economic Theory. *Yale Journal on Regulation* 38 (2): 480–502.

Ash, Elliott, Daniel L. Chen, and Suresh Naidu. 2021. Ideas Have Consequences: The Impact of Law and Economics on American Justice. Unpublished paper, March.

Baker, Jonathan B. 2019. *The Antitrust Paradigm: Restoring a Competitive Economy*. Cambridge, Massachusetts: Harvard University Press.

Barton, Benjamin H., and Stephen Bibas. 2017. *Rebooting Justice: More Technology, Fewer Lawyers, and the Future of Law*. New York: Encounter Books.

Baude, Will. 2019. In Defense of "Virtual Briefing" (i.e., Blogging, Tweeting, Podcasting About Supreme Court Cases). *The Volokh Conspiracy*, May 29.

Beioley, Kate. 2022. London's "Magic Circle" Law Firms Make Renewed Bid to Crack US. *Financial Times*, August 9.

Berrey, Ellen, Steve G. Hoffman, and Laura Beth Nielsen. 2012. Situated Justice: A Contextual Analysis of Fairness and Inequality in Employment Discrimination Litigation. *Law & Society Review* 46 (1): 1–36.

Bonica, Adam. 2020. Why Are There so Many Lawyers in Congress? *Legislative Studies Quarterly* 45 (May): 253–289.

Bonica, Adam, and Maya Sen. 2021. Estimating Judicial Ideology. *Journal of Economic Perspectives* 35 (Winter): 97–118.

Bork, Robert H. 1971. Neutral Principles and Some First Amendment Problems. *Indiana Law Journal* 47 (Fall): 1–61.

Bowie, Nikolas. 2021. The Contemporary Debate over Supreme Court Reform: Origins and Perspectives. Presidential Commission on the Supreme Court of the United States, June 30.

Bazelon, Emily. 2015. Better Judgment. *New York Times Magazine*, June 21.

Bromwich, Jonah E. 2022. Family Court Lawyers Flee Low-Paying Jobs. Parents and Children Suffer. *New York Times*, April 29.

Bump, Philip. 2021. Amy Coney Barrett Assures America That Partisanship in One Step Removed from the Supreme Court. *Washington Post*, September 13.

Butler, Paul. 2021. Kyle Rittenhouse's $2 Million Legal Funds Won His Case. Most Defendants Can't Afford that Quality of Aid. *Washington Post*, November 21.
Carroll, Sidney L., and Robert J. Gaston. 1981. Occupational Restrictions and the Quality of Service Received: Some Evidence. *Southern Economic Journal* 47 (April): 959–976.
Cassens Weiss, Debra. 2023. Bar Admission Denied for Applicant who Rose to Law Firm Partnership Without Law License. *ABA Journal*, June 6.
Chemerinsky, Erwin. 2022. *Worse Than Nothing: The Dangerous Fallacy of Originalism*. New Haven, Connecticut: Yale University Press.
Chemerinsky, Erwin. 2021. Precedent Seems to Matter Little in the Roberts Court. *ABA Journal*, June 3. https://www.abajournal.com/columns/article/chemerinsky-precedent-seems-to-matter-little-in-the-roberts-court.
Chemerinsky, Erwin. 2014. *The Case Against the Supreme Court*. New York: Viking Press.
Choi, Jonathan H., and Daniel Schwarz. 2023. AI Assistance in Legal Analysis: An Empirical Study. Minnesota Legal Studies Research Paper No. 23-22.
Cohen, Alma. 2023. The Pervasive Influence of Ideology at the Federal Circuit Courts. NBER Working Paper No. 31509, July.
Cohen, Alma, and Crystal S. Yang. 2019. Judicial Politics and Sentencing Decisions. *American Economic Journal: Economic Policy* 11 (February): 160–191.
Corrigan, Jack. 2019. VA Released Millions of People's Personal Data Despite Known Risks. *Nextgov*, November 18.
Cotton, Michele. 2017. Improving Access to Justice by Enforcing the Free Speech Clause. *Brooklyn Law Review* 83: 111–156.
Crandall, Robert W., and Clifford Winston. 2003. Does Antitrust Policy Improve Consumer Welfare? Assessing the Evidence. *Journal of Economic Perspectives* 17 (Fall): 3–26.
Cunniffe, Christopher T. 1997. The Case for the Alternative Third-Year Program. *Albany Law Review* 61 (1): 85–145.
Dagan, Hanoch, and Roy Kreitner. 2021. Economic Analysis in Law. *Yale Journal on Regulation* 38 (2): 566–588.
Devins, Neal, and Lawrence Baum. 2017. Split Definitive: How Party Polarization Turned the Supreme Court Into a Partisan Court. *Supreme Court Law Review* 216: 301–363.
Deming, David J., Michael L. Lovenheim, and Richard W. Patterson. 2016. The Competitive Effects of Online Education." NBER Working Paper 22749, October.
Dube, Arindrajit. 2024. Response. *Journal of Political Economy Microeconomics*, forthcoming.

Engstrom, David Freeman, Lucy Ricca, Graham Ambrose, and Maddie Walsh. 2022. *Legal Innovation After Reform: Evidence from Regulatory Change*, Deborah L. Rhode Center on the Legal Profession, Stanford Law School, September. https://law.stanford.edu/wp-content/uploads/2022/09/SLS-CLP-Regulatory-Reform-REPORTExecSum-9.26.pdf.

Epstein, Lee, William Landes, and Richard Posner. 2013. How Business Fares in the Supreme Court. *Minnesota Law Review* 97: 1431–1472.

Epstein, Richard. 2013. The Myth of a Pro-Business SCOTUS. Hoover Institution, Stanford University, July 9. www.hoover.org/research/myth-pro-business-scotus.

Esposito, Christopher, Jerry Nickelsburg, and Edward E. Leamer. 2021. Who Paid Los Angeles' Minimum Wage? A Side-By-Side Minimum Wage Experiment in Los Angeles County. NBER Working Paper 28966, June.

Farranato, Chiara, Andrey Fradkin, Bradley J. Larsen, and Erik Brynjolfsson. 2024. Consumer Protection in an Online World: An Analysis of Occupational Licensing. *American Economic Journal: Applied Economics* 16 (July): 549–579.

Fisher, Jeffrey L., and Allison Orr Larsen. 2019. Virtual Briefing at the Supreme Court. *Cornell Law Review* 105: 85–136.

Flood, John, and Lachlan Robb. 2018. Professions and Expertise: How Machine Learning and Blockchain are Redesigning the Landscape of Professional Knowledge and Organization. Griffith Law School Research Paper No. 18-20.

Friedman, Milton. 1962. *Capitalism and Freedom*. Chicago, Illinois: University of Chicago Press.

Gibney, Bruce Cannon. 2019. *The Nonsense Factory: The Making and Breaking of the American Legal System*. New York: Hachette Books.

Gillers, Stephen. 2014. Lowering the Bar: How Lawyer Discipline in New York Fails to Protect the Public. *Legislation and Public Policy* 17: 485–541.

Goodman, Joshua, Julia Melkers, and Amanda Pallais. 2017. Can Online Delivery Increase Access to Education? NBER Working Paper 22754, September.

Gorsuch, Neil M., and Janie Nitze. 2024. *Over Ruled: The Human Toll of Too Much Law*. New York: HarperCollins.

Gorsuch, Neil M. with Jane Nitze and David Feder. 2019. *A Republic, If You Can Keep It*. New York: Penguin Random House.

Guzman, Hugo. 2023. In-House Attorneys Don't Trust Their Understanding of AI—and Thus Most Aren't Using It. *Law.Com*, October 2.

Hadfield, Gillian K. 2010. Higher Demand, Lower Supply? A Comparative Assessment of the Legal Resource Landscape for Ordinary Americans. *Fordham Urban Law Journal* 37: 129–156.

Hadfield, Gillian K. 2022. Legal Markets. *Journal of Economic Literature* 60 (December): 1264–1315.

Harris, Barnett J. 2022. Protecting the P(ocket)UBLIC: Why the Legal Professions Regulation/Shmegulation is Truly Just All About the Benjamins. *Houston Law Review* 12: 60–75.

Hemel, Daniel. 2021. Can Structural Changes Fix the Supreme Court? *Journal of Economic Perspectives* 35 (Winter): 119–142.

Henderson, Todd. 2017. Do Lawyers Make Better CEOs than MBAs? *Harvard Business Review*, August 24.

Henderson, William. 2017. The Legal Profession's Last Mile Solution. *Law.Com*, July 10.

Hirschman, Albert O. 1970. *Exit, Voice, and Loyalty*. Cambridge, Massachusetts: Harvard University Press.

Howard, Philip K. 2023. *Everyday Freedom: Designing the Framework for a Flourishing Society*. New York: Rodin Books.

Howard, Philip K. 2019. Bureaucracy vs. Democracy: Examining the Bureaucratic Causes of Public Failure, Economic Waste, and Voter Alienation. *The American Interest*, January 31. www.the-american-interest.com/2019/01/31/bureaucracy-vs-democracy.

Howarth, Joan. 2022. *Shaping the Bar: The Future of Attorney Licensing*. Redwood City: Stanford University Press.

Jha, Priyaranjan, David Neumark, and Antonio Rodriguez-Lopez. 2024. What's Across the Border? Re-evaluating the Cross-Border Evidence on Minimum Wage Effects. *Journal of Political Economy Microeconomics*, forthcoming.

Johnson, Janna E., and Morris M. Kleiner. 2020. Is Occupational Licensing a Barrier to Interstate Migration? *American Economic Journal: Economic Policy* 12 (August): 347–373.

Karabarbounis, Loukas, Jeremy Lise, and Anusha Nath. 2022. Minimum Wages and Labor Markets in the Twin Cities. NBER Working Paper 30239, July.

Katz, Michael L. 2021. How to Fix the Courts' Misuse of Economics. *Promarket*, December 7. https://promarket.org/2021/12/07/courts-economics-antitrust-consumer-welfare/.

Kearney, Joseph D., and Thomas W. Merrill. 2000. The Influence of Amicus Curiae Briefs on the Supreme Court. *University of Pennsylvania Law Review* 148 (January): 743–855.

Khan, Lina M. 2017. Amazon's Antitrust Paradox. *Yale Law Journal* 126 (3): 710–805.

Kleiner, Morris, and Evgeny S. Vorotnikov. 2018. *At What Cost? State and National Estimates of the Cost of Occupational Licensing*. Washington, D.C.: Institute for Justice. https://ij.org/wp-content/uploads/2018/11/Licensure%20Report%20WEB.pdf.

Kleiner, Morris M., and Robert T. Kudrle. 2000. Does Regulation Affect Economic Outcomes? The Case of Dentistry. *Journal of Law and Economics* 43 (October): 547–582.

Knake, Renee Newman. 2018. The Legal Monopoly. *Washington Law Review* 93: 1294–1338.
Knowles Myers, Caitlin, and Morgan Welch. 2021. What Can Economic Research Tell Us About The Effect of Abortion Access on Women's Lives? Washington, DC: Brookings Institution. https://www.brookings.edu/research/what-can-economic-research-tell-us-about-the-effect-of-abortion-access-on-womens-lives/.
Kronman, Anthony T. 1993. *The Lost Lawyer: Failing Ideals of the Legal Profession.* Cambridge, Massachusetts: Harvard University Press.
Lazarus, Richard J. 2021. Advocacy History in the Supreme Court. *The Supreme Court Review* 2020: 423–466.
Legal Services Corporation. 2017. The Justice Gap: Measuring the Unmet Civil Legal Needs of Low-income Americans. NORC at the University of Chicago for Legal Services Corporation. www.lsc.gov/sites/default/files/images/TheJusticeGap-FullReport.pdf.
Leong, Brenda, and Patrick Hall. 2021. 5 Things Lawyers Should Know About Artificial Intelligence. *ABA Journal*, December 14.
Levine, Michael E. 1989. Comment. *Brookings Papers on Economic Activity: Microeconomics*, 42–48.
Levine, Michael E. 1965. Is Regulation Necessary? California Air Transportation and National Regulatory Policy. *Yale Law Journal* 74: 1416–1447.
Liptak, Adam. 2018. A Case for Math, not "Gobbledygook" in Judging Partisan Voting Maps. *New York Times*, January 15.
Liptak, Adam. 2017. An Exit Interview with Richard Posner, Judicial Provocateur. *New York Times*, September 11.
Litan, Robert E. 2014. *Trillion Dollar Economists.* Hoboken, New Jersey: Wiley.
Love, Bruce. 2022. Another Two SEC Lawyers Defect—This Time to Wilkie. *National Law Journal*, July 5.
MacEwen, Bruce, and Janet Stanton. 2017. *What Makes the Elite NYC Legal Market so Different?* New York: Adam Smith, Esq.
Martin, Lauren, Nick Whitehouse, Stephanie Yiu, Lizzie Catterson, and Rivindu Perera. 2024. Better Call GPT, Comparing Large Language Models Against Lawyers. Unpublished paper. https://arxiv.org/pdf/2401.16212.pdf.
Matter, Ulrich, and Alois Stutzer. 2015. The Role of Lawyer-Legislators in Shaping the Law: Evidence from Voting on Tort Reforms. *Journal of Law and Economics* 58 (2): 357–384.
McDonald, R. Robin. 2019. GA. Justices Hone in on Discovery, Statistical Anomalies in Lt. Governor's Election Fight. *Law.Com*, May 7.
Michaels, Dave. 2022. Federal Antitrust Lawyers Seek to Reverse Lackluster Trial Record. *Wall Street Journal*, June 5.
Miller, Joe. 2024a. Diverse Lawyers Used as 'Window Dressing' in Client Pitches, Poll Finds. *Financial Times*, July 14.

Miller, Joe. 2024b. Partner Pay at Top US Law Firms Jumps to Record $1.4mn, *Financial Times*, October 24.

Miller, Mark C. 1995. *The High Priests of American Politics: The Role of Lawyers in American Political Institutions*. Knoxville: University of Tennessee Press.

Miller, Sarah, Laura R. Wherry, and Diana Greene Foster. 2023. The Economic Consequences of Being Denied an Abortion. *American Economic Journal: Economic Policy* 15 (February): 394–437.

Najmabadi, Shannon. 2023. Courts Come to Order With Judges, Litigants—But No Lawyers. *Wall Street Journal*, October 7.

National Center for State Courts. 2015. Civil Justice Initiative: The Landscape of Civil Litigation in State Courts. www.ncsc.org/~/media/Files/PDF/Research/CivilJusticeReport-2015.ashx.

Noll, Roger G. 1989. Comment. *Brookings Papers on Economic Activity: Microeconomics*, 48–58.

Olson, Elizabeth. 2016. When Finding the Right Lawyer Seems Daunting, Crowdsource One. *New York Times*, December 28.

Packel, Dan. 2021. Two Steps Forward, One Step Back: The Year in Legal Industry Regulatory Reform. *Law.Com*, December 23.

Peltzman, Sam. 1976. Toward a More General Theory of Regulation. *Journal of Law and Economics* 19 (August): 211–240.

Peltzman, Sam. 1989. The Economic Theory of Regulation after a Decade of Deregulation. *Brookings Papers on Economic Activity: Microeconomics*, 1–41.

Posner, Richard A. 2013. *Reflections on Judging*. Cambridge, Massachusetts: Harvard University Press.

Posner, Richard A. 2008. *How Judges Think*. Cambridge, Massachusetts: Harvard University Press.

Posner, Richard A. 1995. *Overcoming Law*. Cambridge, Massachusetts: Harvard University Press.

Posner, Richard A. 1987. The Decline of Law as an Autonomous Discipline: 1962–1987. *Harvard Law Review* 100 (February): 761–780.

Re, Richard M. 2023. Personal Precedent at the Supreme Court. *Harvard Law Review* 136 (3): 824–860.

Reynolds, Matt. 2023a. 2023 *Profile of the Legal Profession* Report Spotlights the Scarcity of Legal Aid Lawyers. *ABA Journal*, November 30.

Reynolds, Matt. 2023b. Majority of Lawyers Have no Immediate Plans to Use Generative AI, LexisNexis Survey Finds. *ABA Journal*, March 24.

Reynolds, Matt. 2023c. How ChatGPT and Other AI Platforms Could Dramatically Reshape the Legal Industry. *ABA Journal*, June 1.

Rhode, Deborah L. 2004. *Access to Justice*. Oxford, United Kingdom: Oxford University Press.

Rozema, Kyle. 2021. Does the Bar Exam Protect the Public? *Journal of Empirical Legal Studies* 18: 801–848.

Rozema, Kyle. 2023. How Do Occupational Licensing Requirements Affect Labor Supply? Evidence from the Legal Profession, June. SSRN: https://ssrn.com/abstract=.

Rozema, Kyle. 2024. Professional Discipline and the Labor Market: Evidence from Lawyers. *Journal of Law and Economics*, forthcoming. https://papers.ssrn.com/sol3/papers.cfm?abstract_id=4381417.

Schrager, Allison. 2024. What Do Graduates of Yale Law School Know About Economics? *Bloomberg*, August 5.

Schuck, Peter H. 2014. *Why Government Fails So Often: And How It Can Do Better*. Princeton, New Jersey: Princeton University Press.

Scott, Robert E., and George D. Triantis. 2021. What Do Lawyers Contribute to Law and Economics? *Yale Journal on Regulation* 38 (2): 707–731.

Shapiro, Carl. 2019. Protecting Competition in the American Economy: Merger Control, Tech Titans, Labor Markets. *Journal of Economic Perspectives* 33 (Summer): 69–93.

Simon, Michael, Alvin F. Lindsay, Loly Sosa, and Paige Comparato. 2018. Lola v. Skadden and the Automation of the Legal Profession. *Yale Journal of Law and Technology* 20: 234–310.

Smith, Patrick. 2022a. Bring in the Pros: To Keep Key Clients, Firms Are Turning to Business Expertise. *National Law Journal*, March 10.

Smith, Patrick. 2022b. These Firms Dominated 2021 M&A League Tables. *National Law Journal*, January 5.

Stacey, Kiran. 2021. Washington vs Big Tech: Lina Khan's Battle to Transform American Antitrust. *Financial Times*, August 10.

Stigler, George J. 1971. The Theory of Economic Regulation. *Bell Journal of Economics and Management Science* 2 (Spring): 3–21.

Strohl, Jeff, Catherine Morris, and Ban Cheah. 2024. *A Law Degree Is No Sure Thing: Some Law School Graduates Earn Top Dollar, but Many Do Not*. Washington, DC: Georgetown University Center on Education and the Workforce, http://www.cew.georgetown.edu/law.

Thompson, Neil C., Brian Flanagan, Edana Richardson, Brian McKenzie, and Xueyun Luo. 2024. Trial by Internet: A Randomized Field Experiment on Wikipedia's Influence on Judges' Legal Reasoning. In *The Cambridge Handbook of Experimental Jurisprudence*. UK: Cambridge University Press, forthcoming.

Thomson Reuters. 2022. *Overcoming Lawyers' Resistance to Change*. Legal Global product. https://legal.thomsonreuters.com/en/insights/articles/overcoming-lawyers-resistance-to-change.

Vanderford, Richard. 2022. Law Firms Branch Out Beyond Lawyers in Bid to Beat Out Rival Advisers. *Wall Street Journal*, May 28.

Verma, Pranshu, and Will Oremus. 2023. These Lawyers Used ChatGPT to Save Time. They Got Fired and Fined. *Washington Post*, November 16.

Vermuele, Adrian. 2022. There Is No Conservative Legal Movement. *Washington Post*, July 6.

Villasenor, John. 2022. Why Law Professors Should Co-author Academic Articles with Law Students. *ABA Journal*, June 22.

Ward, Stephanie Francis. 2022. Following Decades of Discourse on Nonlawyer Legal Services, Questions of Motives Continue. *ABA Journal*, August 17.

Winston, Clifford. 1993. Economic Deregulation: Days of Reckoning for Microeconomists. *Journal of Economic Literature* 31 (September): 1263–1289.

Winston, Clifford. 1998. US Industry Adjustment to Economic Deregulation. *Journal of Economic Perspectives* 12 (Summer): 89–110.

Winston, Clifford. 2006. *Government Failure Versus Market Failure: Microeconomics Policy Research and Government Performance*. Washington, D.C.: AEI-Brookings Institution Press.

Winston, Clifford. 2021a. *Gaining Ground: Markets Helping Government*. Washington, DC: Brookings Institution Press.

Winston, Clifford. 2021b. Back to the Good—Or Were They the Bad—Old Days of Antitrust? A Review Essay of Jonathan B. Baker's *The Antitrust Paradigm: Restoring a Competitive Economy*. *Journal of Economic Literature* 59 (1): 265–284.

Winston, Clifford, and Quentin Karpilow. 2016. Should the U.S. Eliminate Entry Barriers to the Practice of Law? Perspectives Shaped by Industry Deregulation. *American Economic Review Papers and Proceedings* 5 (May): 171–176.

Winston, Clifford, David Burk, and Jia Yan. 2021. *Trouble at the Bar: An Economics Perspective on the Legal Profession and the Case for Fundamental Reform*. Washington, DC: Brookings Institution Press.

Winston, Clifford, Robert W. Crandall, and Vikram Maheshri. 2011. *First Thing We Do, Let's Deregulate All the Lawyers*. Washington, DC: Brookings Institution Press.

Wu, Tim. 2018. *The Curse of Bigness: Antitrust in the New Gilded Age*. New York: Columbia University Press, Columbia Global Reports.

CHAPTER 3

Is Deregulating the Medical Profession Just What the Doctor Ordered?

Conor Norris, Robert Orr, and Edward Timmons

Abstract The United States faces a shortage of medical providers. In this chapter, we argue that this shortage has been caused by stringent regulation of the medical profession. We summarize physician regulation in the United States and provide comparisons with physician regulations in other developed nations. We then argue that occupational licensing in its present form is costly and insufficient to protect patients. We conclude by

---

We are grateful to Alex Tabarrok and Clifford Winston for providing excellent comments on earlier drafts of this chapter.

C. Norris (✉) · E. Timmons
West Virginia University, Morgantown, WV, USA
e-mail: conor.norris@mail.wvu.edu

E. Timmons
e-mail: edward.timmons@mail.wvu.edu

R. Orr
Niskanen Center, Washington DC, USA

© The Author(s), under exclusive license to Springer Nature Switzerland AG 2024
C. Winston (ed.), *Reforming Occupational Licensing in the US*,
https://doi.org/10.1007/978-3-031-74349-8_3

presenting alternative ways to regulate the medical profession that will be less costly and will not compromise the quality of patient care.

Keywords Medical profession · Occupational licensing · Certification · Scope of practice

1 Introduction

The prevailing healthcare discussion in the United States today mistakenly focuses on fairness and equity, accepting a persistent shortage of necessary resources and attempting to devise methods to ration them. We reject this premise entirely; instead, we argue for expanding healthcare supply, increasing the number of physicians, and utilizing our current healthcare resources in a way that increases access to care. Going back decades, the political debate on healthcare has focused primarily on providing insurance to make healthcare more affordable. But what good is health insurance if patients are unable to find a physician? Difficulty accessing care is not just inconvenient for patients, it worsens their health outcomes. Trying to improve access by subsidizing demand for healthcare while simultaneously limiting the supply of professionals is a recipe for increasing both spending and patient dissatisfaction with healthcare.

Indeed, the United States has been facing a shortage of physicians since the 2000s and this situation is not expected to improve. Primary care, which is most patients' interaction with healthcare, faces a more dire situation. Currently, the United States is estimated to be 13,700 primary care physicians short of the preferred minimum threshold of primary care physicians per patient (IHS Markit 2021). This shortage will persist and because of a growing demand from an aging population, physicians opting for higher-paying specialties, and perhaps most importantly barriers to entry into the medical profession that prevent the supply of physicians from responding to market demand, the shortfall of primary care physicians is projected to grow to between 17,800 and 48,000 by 2034.

But these estimates don't tell the whole story of how bad the situation is in the United States. The United States has 2.7 physicians per 1000 residents, just 4 countries in the OECD (Turkey, Mexico, South Korea, and Japan) have fewer physicians per capita (OECD 2023). Every country in the EU has considerably more physicians per capita than the United States, and Austria and Norway have about double. Considering that physicians in the United States earn considerably more than their OECD counterparts, it may seem puzzling that this relative shortage exists and shows no sign of reversing (Gottlieb et al. 2023). Economists espouse that relatively high wages in a field will attract more workers, over time decreasing their wages. Unsurprisingly, government regulations stand in the way. And even less surprisingly, physicians tend to support restrictions that maintain their earnings. Who can blame them?

Unlike most professions, the practice of medicine is overseen by multiple institutions. State medical boards issue licenses to physicians who meet their entry requirements and discipline physicians who provide substandard care. The American Medical Association (AMA) does not have direct regulatory authority, but it can influence state and federal healthcare policy and education standards (Friedman 1962). The specialty societies governing the various physician specializations (for example, the American Board of Dermatology) are the more pertinent source of pseudo-regulatory authority, promulgating entry requirements as well as stipulating best practices in terms of clinical practice patterns. While the specialty societies are nominally private, their judgments effectively often approach statutory public law in practice. The judgments of specialty societies are utilized by institutions like the malpractice litigation system and hospital accreditors that also regulate the practice of medicine. The accreditation of medical residency training programs is overseen by the Accreditation Council on Graduate Medical Education (ACGME) for graduate medical training programs. These institutions combine to protect patients and ensure they receive quality care from competent physicians.

Collectively, these institutions create formidable entry barriers for individuals who wish to practice medicine.[1] The fundamental issue about such occupational licensing is whether its benefits justify its costs or whether fundamental reform of entry into the practice of medicine would significantly improve access to healthcare and benefit the public.

One can imagine the entry restrictions on physicians improving the quality of physicians and improving patient health outcomes. But one

---

[1] Other entry barriers to medical practice include poorly designed limitations on residency position funding, immigration policies, and the idiosyncratic structure of US medical education.

can also imagine a scenario where entry restrictions reduce the supply of physicians well below what is optimal for patients. Patients end up having difficulty accessing care, suffering through longer wait times or being forced to drive hours to the nearest physician. Patients delay care and physicians are forced to rush through visits, both of which harm patients. Limited access to physicians, and regulations that prevent other healthcare professionals from providing primary care increase healthcare spending, which would impact low-income patients the most (Osborn et al. 2016).

The purpose of this chapter is to explore the web of physician regulations and to offer more efficient and equitable alternatives to better achieve the same goals that the regulations seek to accomplish. The fundamental public policy question is how we can achieve greater entry into the medical profession, reducing the prices of and expanding access to medical services, while at the same time maintaining high-quality care and protecting patients from malpractice. Licensing alone fails to protect patients against substandard medicine, and at the very least, it can be reformed to decrease prices and increase access. We recognize that medical licensing reforms can appear to be radical at first glance, but as we show, our reforms would be a relatively modest change, allowing most of the current patient protections to remain in place. Instead of onerous regulations, market-based reforms like moving from licensing to certification as the method of professional regulation would be preferable. If occupational licensing must be retained in its current form, reforming residency, combining undergraduate and university medical education into a single degree, and greater utilization of other healthcare professions can offset many of the downsides of licensing.

2 How Licensing Restricts the Supply of Professionals

Consumers struggle to distinguish whether some services will be of high or low quality before receiving them. Economists call this an information asymmetry because the supplier, or service provider, has much more information about the quality of the product or service than the consumer. In a market for services, like medical care, consumers suffer from a disadvantage because compared with the provider, they have much less information about the quality of care that they are likely to receive. Accurately discerning the quality of care provided by a physician is nearly impossible for the typical patient, and as a result they oftentimes rely on unrelated qualities like bedside manner (Hyman et al. 2022). In fact, even patient reviews are not able to identify the physicians who most frequently harm patients through negligence or lack of skills (Hyman et al. 2022). Thus, some form of regulation is necessary to protect patients against physicians with a track record of harm.

The practice of medicine was one of the first professions to require a license. As noted, such licensing appeared to be justified because of the information asymmetry and the risk of physical harm from low-quality service providers. To obtain a license, aspiring professionals must apply to the licensing board, demonstrating their quality by meeting certain requirements, which typically include degrees that require completion of specific courses and subject matters, hands-on training from experienced professionals, passing comprehensive exams that cover the information necessary for independent practice, and requirements that ensure the professionals good character and trustworthiness.

Three different types of potential professionals are intentionally excluded: less highly credentialed medical professionals, unscientific quacks, and outright con men. The popularity of quack healer movements, such as homeopathy and Thomsonian medicine was historically a primary motivator of licensing regulation (Starr 2017). While such quacks do not always pose a direct health risk to consumers, the inability of consumers to assess the efficacy of medical techniques entails that a quack utilizing benign techniques harms the public to the extent that their services crowd out more efficacious clinical practices derived from science. By restricting medical practice to those who have received a medical degree and demonstrated competence, licensing appears to reduce the need for consumers to be experts themselves.

For licensing to be most effective, however, consumers must recognize that it improves quality. When consumers have difficulties or are unable to discern the quality of a professional before purchasing their service, signaling by professionals, which may be costly to obtain but clearly visible, can be beneficial to consumers because it conveys useful information about the professional's quality. Consumers can participate in the market with greater confidence and peace of mind because they can screen out lower-quality service providers who fail to earn the signal. Better-informed consumers will increase the demand for medical services.

Supporters of licensing believe that those who are excluded by licensing requirements will be limited to just the low-quality providers who lack the ability to meet them. However, in practice, licensing laws discourage a portion of those who do have the necessary skills, reducing the competition that current professionals face and patient access to medical services. Self-interested professionals often lobby directly for licensing laws, which make it more difficult for new professionals to enter even if they could provide high-quality services (Friedman 1962). Meanwhile, those already practicing are "grandfathered-in," or exempted from meeting the new licensing requirements. Limiting new competitors can help professionals earn economic rents, or profits greater than the market would allow them to earn. The rent-seeking perspective of licensing posits that licensing exacerbates problems rather than solving them. In this view, licensing boards resemble medieval guilds, primarily protecting their professions from potential competitors and increasing their earnings instead of protecting consumers from harm (Kleiner 2015). It is therefore not surprising that economists, who have been studying the effects of occupational licensing of various professions, consistently find evidence that occupational licensing reduces employment in licensed professions (Kleiner 2006). For example, Blair and Chung estimate that licensing laws reduce employment by 27 percent (Blair and Chung 2019). As a further discouragement to enter the profession, the average medical school graduate has amassed over $200,000 in student loans during the course of their education (AAMC 2023). And spending 4 years in medical school and 3 years in residencies forces physicians to forego years of earnings, encouraging some to opt for a non-licensed high-paying field instead.

The rent-seeking and asymmetric information perspectives are not mutually exclusive. Both Sam Peltzman and Keith Leffler stress that interest groups, like medical associations and state medical boards, can use regulation to simultaneously achieve multiple goals (Peltzman 1976; Leffler 1978). It is doubtful that all but the most self-interested professionals would not care about the general quality of the services offered by their profession, even if the overarching intention was to maximize their own well-being and professional status. Professions throughout human history have sought to utilize legislation as a means of shielding themselves from competition (Plemmons and Timmons 2021). At the same time, medical practices derived from scientific discovery processes have also historically struggled to differentiate themselves from various forms of traditional and folk therapies in the eyes of patients. So, while professional regulation of the practice of medicine may protect physicians from competition and limit access to medical services, history also tells us it can be useful to protect patients from harm (Law and Kim 2005).

3 How Medical Licensing Works

Professional licenses in the healthcare industry generally grant two types of privileges to their holders: "protection of title" and "scope of practice." For physicians, protection of title prevents those without a medical license from advertising themselves using the title of doctor. It is worth noting here that the use of the term "doctor" colloquially is more closely associated with the physician profession rather than other doctorate-degree-holding professions. In California, the title of "doctor" is restricted to licensed physicians only; violators commit a misdemeanor (CA 2054). Indiana passed similar restrictions in 2022 (Avi-Yonah 2023).

The second authorization relates to performing medical services within a specified scope, or scope of practice. For physicians, licenses provide broad authorization to provide medical services, including the authority to prescribe medicine (Graboyes and Feldstein 2021). The broad authority granted under the physician license does not exempt the profession from additional legal and regulatory constraints. For instance, physicians and other healthcare professionals granted prescribing authority as part of their license must also apply with the Drug Enforcement Administration if they plan on prescribing controlled substances. Apart from statutory regulation, constraints on the medical services a physician can actually perform also are imposed by institutions such as accreditors and the malpractice litigation system. Physicians also must receive board certification related to their specialty from the associated member of the American Board of Medical Specialties to obtain hospital privileges.

In sum, there are many medically related authorities that supplement state medical licensing. This distinguishes medical licensing in the United States, in comparison with other countries, as exercising more control over the scope of practice of medicine. The United States often restricts even simple tasks from being legally performed by individuals with entry- or mid-level licenses, as each designated specialty is strictly defined by its licensed scope of practice. Furthermore, these rules differ significantly across states, resulting in a complex and inconsistent regulatory landscape.

In contrast, medical licensing in Europe is less rigid in controlling the scope of practice. For example, in Sweden, although some tasks, such as prescribing medicine, can be executed only by members of certain professional categories, healthcare workers do not need a license to perform tasks like filling a tooth cavity, operating an X-ray machine (or interpreting the results), inserting a urinary catheter, or taking blood samples. Interestingly, Sweden's residency requirements for physicians are shorter than the United States, just 18–24 months. However, there is variation across the European continent. While Germany joins Sweden with just 1–3 years of residency for physicians, France and Greece require 3–6 years like the United States.

The more hands-off approach to licensure practiced in many European countries contrasts sharply with the situation in the United States, where tasks and responsibilities are strictly assigned based on professional license. As a result, the United States requires a much larger share of its healthcare workers to obtain a license compared with Europe (Hermansen 2019). Another consequence of less prescriptive licensing is that there are far fewer distinct occupations that need to be licensed separately. To illustrate, whereas the US state of Virginia's Department of Health licenses 62 distinct healthcare professions, Sweden's National Board of Health and Welfare licenses only 22 distinct occupations (Socialsty Relsen 2022; Virginia DHP 2023). By using more general, broader licensure categories that encompass various distinct modes of task specialization as well as differing levels of education and training, Sweden has found a way of making entry barriers negligible while allowing healthcare workers to be identified and held accountable. There is a clear mechanism of license revocation in the event that such workers pose a danger to patients. This difference reflects Sweden's different understanding of what purpose licensure actually serves compared with common perceptions in the United States. Whereas occupational licensure's primary purpose is generally understood to be gatekeeping in the United States, other countries view it more as a means of identification and accountability.[2]

As predicted by Friedman, rigid restrictions on what constitutes "medical practice" have resulted in new licensed medical professionals to fill the gap, which could be filled by less-credentialed but equally skilled individuals (Friedman 1962). Unsurprisingly, the AMA and state medical associations focus on protecting physicians from competition from these other licensed medical professions, in the name of protecting patients. Physician

---

[2] In Sweden, the term for occupational licensure is "legitimation", which in English more accurately translates as "identification". Given that the English term "license" is broadly understood as a synonym for "permission", it can be fairly said that these semantic differences reflect a different understanding of the purpose of occupational licensure.

groups vigorously oppose any independence for other healthcare professionals, like nurse practitioners and physician assistants, notwithstanding a preponderance of evidence that both professions are fully capable of providing high-quality care that is consistent with their education and training (Bae & Timmons 2022). In the rare cases where they may provide lower quality care than physicians, it occurs when they are asked to perform care outside of their areas of training (Chan and Chen 2022).[3]

The use of licensing laws to protect physicians from competition from other healthcare providers is not a recent invention, it dates back to the early days of medical licensing. In the early 1900s, to increase the usage of obstetricians at births instead of midwives, professional medical associations began a public campaign to discredit and ban the practice of midwifery. The movement was not a result of any medical discovery, rather it was to improve the status of obstetricians among physicians, increase their income by reducing competition from lower-cost providers, and to allow for more training, which physicians openly admitted in medical journals and medical association meetings (Gibson 2016). Where outright banning of midwives was not possible, they devised another plan: use licensing to limit new entry. The plan called for the creation of a midwife license, grandfathering in practicing midwives, and creating standards that would prevent the issuing of any new licenses (Emmons and Huntington 1911). Strict education standards set far in excess of what was necessary would be used to prevent new midwives from being able to obtain a license. Physicians coupled this with a publicity campaign to arouse public sentiment against midwives.

4 Early History American Medical Licensure

How did medical licensure develop in the United States to become such a formidable entry barrier? The US process of adopting medical licensure was slower and bumpier compared with many other countries. Whereas France and many German-speaking states had firmly established traditions of medical regulation well prior to the United States' founding, the

---

[3] For instance, Chan and Chen (2022) find evidence that NPs provide lower quality care in emergency settings in Veterans Administration hospitals. However, the NPs in the study were primarily trained for primary care, not emergency care. We would expect clinicians, whether NPs or physicians, to perform worse in specialties outside of their experience and training.

philosophy toward governance that Americans inherited from the British was more skeptical of a government's role in this sphere. Despite these cultural headwinds, Anglo countries had gradually been moving toward the adoption of limited or locally based forms of medical licensure since the Enlightenment period. Although scientifically informed medicine was still in a nascent state during this era, an increasing number of individuals in English-speaking countries had become convinced that its clinical superiority over folk and traditional approaches was not simply a matter of opinion but an objective reality that governments ought to recognize.

As American physicians trained in major American cities, such as Philadelphia, began to disseminate across the country, momentum toward regularizing the profession around these practices began to build, leading to the passage and enforcement of licensure laws in states and cities up until the late 1820s.

However, the Jackson era's populist backlash against monopolism prompted the de-licensure of many professions across the country, including medical professionals (Johnson and Chaudhry 2012). Alternative medical practitioners at odds with the academic medical orthodoxy rose in popularity during this period, such as Thomsonianism, eclecticism, and homeopathy (Duffy 1993). Whether this upsurge in unscientific healers can be attributed to delicensing itself or merely symptomatic of a deeper underlying skepticism toward authority in American culture is hard to say definitively. What's clear is that the trajectory toward medical licensure in the United States had definitively diverged from other English-speaking countries, which continued to regularize and strengthen medical licensure laws during these years. The increasing divergence from places like Canada may have been in part driven by a negative reaction to the trends observed in the United States (along with a dose of Canadian nationalism), with one historian writing that "there were widespread and not unjustified fears that lax enforcement of licensing laws would invite a descent on Canada by battalions of American quacks armed with republicanism as well as charlatanism" (Kett 1967). While England regularized medical licensure standards with the passage of the 1858 Medical Act, the same would not occur in the United States until after the release of the Flexner Report roughly fifty years later (Roberts 2009).

Medical licensure was gradually reestablished in the United States after the Civil War. Populist antipathy toward licensing had begun to wane with the rising economic heft of large-scale corporations increasingly seen as the serious monopolistic threat (Carpenter 2019). But the changing political climate did not immediately result in medical licensure being reestablished. Popularity over the preceding decades of medical approaches derived from nonscientific sources had resulted in internal division over what a common basis for licensure might look like. Many medical institutions were composed of both scientific and, for instance, homeopathic practitioners, and the services that individual physicians performed often drew upon a hybrid of different approaches. For these reasons, medical licensure's reestablishment was initially compromised in formalizing a scientific basis for medical practice, often allowing non-allopaths to receive the license or else carving out separate licensing structures for these groups.[4]

The previously unprecedented accumulations of wealth enabled by the rise of corporations played a significant role in formalizing medical licensure around a scientific basis. As philanthropists of the period became aware of American medicine's backwardness when juxtaposed against the application of laboratory science occurring in Europe, they increasingly devoted sums to professionalizing American medicine around a scientific foundation (Büttner 1992). Among the most impactful of these early investments was the bequest provided following the death of Baltimore businessman Johns Hopkins in 1873, establishing a European-style research university that was fully integrated with a hospital. A few of Johns Hopkins' initial faculty would go on to profoundly shape the course of American medicine. In particular, William Osler and William Welch would play an outsized role, through their formal leadership positions in professional bodies such as the American Medical Association, in advising large philanthropic grant-makers, and providing consultation as part of the highly influential Flexner Report (Shryock 1956).

The release of the Flexner Report in 1911, which decried both the quality and consistency of North American medical instruction and practice, precipitated massive changes across the various institutions governing physician medical practice. Countless medical schools, including five of the seven black medical schools, were shut down or reorganized in

---

[4] Osteopaths largely refused to be integrated into the licensing arrangements of allopaths, sometimes carving out separate quack licenses (along with naturopaths who are still separate). During the 1980s in the United States, osteopaths internally reformed and mainstreamed themselves and then lobbied to get included into the physician license in states where a separate license did not already exist. Interestingly, this mainstreaming of osteopathic medicine never occurred in Europe.

response (Wright-Mendoza 2019). As noted in the previous chapter on the legal profession, racism arguably played a role in licensing lawyers to limit entry into the profession.

5 FSMB Establishment and Geographic Mobility

In 1912, the Federation of State Medical Boards (FSMB) was established as a response to post-Flexner concerns about inconsistent medical licensing practices (Johnson and Chaudhry 2012). While initially committed to reciprocal licensure recognition across state lines, this was ultimately abandoned due to concerns that state boards would undercut each other in terms of fee revenue and thus the degree of workforce oversight they were willing to conduct. Instead, the FSMB opted to merely ensure "endorsement" of credentials obtained across state lines when applying for an in-state license. The basic dynamic that led to the abandonment of physician licensure portability continues to the present day, with physicians required to be licensed in every state that they practice. This flaw in the US licensing regime has become increasingly apparent in recent years as telemedicine use has become more prevalent and patients in one state may be limited from getting telemedicine service from a nearby physician in another state. For example, a physician in Pennsylvania who wants to provide telemedicine to a patient residing just across the border in New Jersey must first obtain a separate license in New Jersey. But this is not ubiquitous; there are some rare cases where states have been willing to recognize licenses from other states. Idaho is one such example. A physician with an active license from any other state is able to provide telemedicine to patients located in Idaho without being forced to obtain an Idaho license, provided the physician has established a relationship with the patient or is employed by an Idaho facility (ID Statutes 54–5713).

Approaches to mitigate cross-state practice issues for doctors using state compacts have thus far fallen short. The current Interstate Medical Licensure Compact merely streamlines the licensing process while leaving intact the need to obtain multiple licenses to practice in multiple states. Indeed, the processing fees increase costs to patients.

In contrast, doctors in Europe are typically licensed at the national level. The countries most streamlined in their licensing process are Scandinavian countries like Sweden and Denmark, which issue licenses for life without the need for many rounds of renewal throughout one's career.

Not only does this allow for seamless practice within countries, but it removes unnecessary headaches and reduces costs for the practitioners and patients. Currently in the United States, more than 22 percent of physicians are licensed in at least two states, and 7 percent have licenses in three or more states (Young et al. 2019). To be licensed in all 50 states, a physician would need to spend over $10,000 in renewal fees every few years. Physicians who hold licenses in multiple states face significantly higher fees than their European counterparts.

6   Licensure and the Residency

By the 1920s, many states were requiring that licensed physicians undergo at least one year of "internship" gaining hands-on clinical experience before they could practice. Often this involved rotating through various areas of clinical service, but "advanced internships" or "residencies" providing an extended, more in-depth experience in a specific clinical field often proliferated during this period.

Initially, this internship requirement was not a substantial barrier to licensure because hospitals' demand for intern labor far outstripped the supply of medical graduates that they were able to take on. Indeed, the intensity of hospitals' demand was seen as the bigger problem, often pressuring medical students to sign commitment contracts earlier and earlier in their medical school tenures (Ludmerer 2014). To address this, the National Intern Matching Program (later renamed the National Resident Matching Program) was established in 1952 as a centralized nonprofit clearinghouse to disarm this dynamic. To illustrate the intensity of this competition from the hospitals' perspective, there were only 5800 medical graduates available to fill roughly 10,500 positions (Mullin and Stalnaker 1951).

Initially, the disparate residency programs were governed by numerous autonomous Residency Review Committees (RRCs) in the individual specialties and subspecialties. But by the early 1970s, calls to regularize and raise standards prompted medical governance institutions to collaborate on the creation of a centralized accrediting body. In 1972, the Liaison Committee for Graduate Medical Education (later reorganized as the Accreditation Council on Graduate Medical Education (ACGME)) was established to oversee the RRCs (Ludmerer 2014). Notably, this body was designated as the gatekeeper to access residency financing through federal programs financing residencies such as Medicare.

The centralization of a residency accrediting authority coincided with the rising standards. In 1975, the option to pursue a rotating internship as a pathway to general practice was eliminated (Ludmerer 2014). From that point onward, physicians looking to pursue a more generalist practice would need to spend at least three years in residency programs, often via internal medicine or the newly created family medicine specialty. ACGME standards continued to rise while federal residency funding became less generous, which caused a shift in power from residents to hospitals such that hospitals were no longer willing or able to take on as many residents as the market could produce (Orr 2021). As a result, many Americans with medical degrees go unmatched each year and countless many more medical graduates of foreign medical schools get passed over for such opportunities entirely.

For physicians receiving their medical residency training abroad, current licensing requirements in all 50 states recognize training that is conducted only at a US- or Canadian-accredited residency. Thus, although in theory, comparatively high physician wages ought to attract accomplished physicians from countries such as the United Kingdom or Switzerland to practice here, in practice, the requirement that these physicians undergo years of redundant training at the compressed wages offered during residency serves as a heavy disincentive to foreign-trained physicians considering practicing in the United States (Gottlieb 2021). Physicians trained in even the most advanced medical systems abroad must start from square-one if they wish to be licensed in the United States.

Modern US residency training blurs the lines between a traditional structured educational program and a paid vocational apprenticeship. Whereas hospital demand for medical residents vastly outstripped the supply of medical graduates when the institution was established over a century ago, regulatory policies reversed the economic fundamentals underlying the institution's training of medical graduates (Orr 2021). Today, admittance into a residency program is highly competitive. Rising program standards and tighter financing and tightening public funding have created an economic dynamic wherein training an additional resident is likely to pencil out as a net-cost for a given teaching facility (Pearse 1983). The most significant of these constraints on public funding for physician training was enacted as part of the 1997 Balanced Budget Act, which capped the number of Medicare-funded residency training slots

(Phillips et al. 2004). The resulting lack of alignment between the profitability of training medical residents at a teaching facility and the health system's broader workforce demands is problematic given the indispensable role that physicians play in the delivery of many healthcare services. Hospitals are hesitant to bear the cost of residencies themselves, because of the availability of federal funds and that the additional costs of self-funding a residency may be passed through in the form of higher hospital prices (Leventhal 2022).

7 Why Licensing is Not Sufficient to Ensure Quality and Access

Compared with other professions, physicians have the most time-consuming and costly licensing requirements. Even after being licensed, physicians have to overcome the additional hurdle of obtaining board certification to practice. State medical boards oversee the practice of medicine, disciplining physicians who offer substandard care. And for all in-patient care, physicians need to obtain the appropriate hospital privileges, and all physicians are required to obtain malpractice insurance. As Friedman argues, relying on state medical boards to oversee practice, a component of physician licensing, may undermine the goal of malpractice insurance to provide safe care because members of the American Medical Association may be unwilling to discredit or harm a fellow member of the association—possibly fearing to be ostracized from the Association (Friedman 1962).

In addition to not fully protecting consumers from harm, licensing also harms patients by reducing access to care. The current system for graduate medical education exacerbates the effects of physician licensing. As noted in the preceding section, residency slots necessary for licensure are limited. The vast majority of residency slots are funded through Medicare. The original intent behind Medicare's financing of residencies was merely to replace similar payments that private insurers had been making on behalf of elderly patients who were newly covered by Medicare (Ludmerer 2014). Over time, however, increasing health insurer competition and declining profit margins made it increasingly difficult for private insurers to pass on resident training costs to consumers via higher premiums (Reuter 1997). As a result, residency programs became increasingly reliant upon Medicare for additional financing.

Medicare's funding was itself limited from the 1980s through the 2000s to prevent a misguided fear of an oversupply of physicians, and subsequent growth has not been enough to catch up to the increase in demand. Additionally, the high costs of medical school encourage physicians to enter more lucrative specialties instead of offering primary care, further reducing access to primary care.

The combination of all the restrictions on medical practice has caused there to be a significant shortfall in access to healthcare in the United States. The US Department of Health and Human Services classifies an area experiencing a shortfall as a Health Professional Shortage Area (HPSA). For primary care, once an area reaches more than 3500 patients for each physician, we classify it as an HPSA. In 2022, 1508 areas were considered an HPSA for primary care. That translates to over 37 million residents in the United States living with insufficient access to care (Kaiser Family Foundation 2021). Physicians tend to cluster in urban and suburban areas, away from rural areas and low-income urban areas. Physicians tend to live near their location of residency, as they have begun to establish a social life and begin raising a family. Additionally, the high cost of medical school discourages physicians from practicing in HPSAs, where physicians tend to earn less.

Difficulty accessing primary care is not simply an inconvenience for patients; it leads to worse health outcomes that ultimately increase healthcare costs for the entire nation (Basu et al. 2019). When patients face longer travel time and driving distances and more time spent in the waiting room, they tend to delay care until it is absolutely necessary. Unfortunately, this allows conditions to worsen and become more difficult to treat. Worsening disease severity lowers the quality of life and even overall life expectancy. A greater number of physicians in a county is associated with lower mortality and a longer mortality-adjusted life expectancy (Basu et al. 2019). Consider recovery from surgery, which requires repeated follow-up appointments. We have evidence that children living in HPSAs have a lower 10-year survival rate after surgery because of the more limited access to care and the difficulties of making it to appointments (Shifman et al. 2022). Delays in first getting a diagnosis and more missed appointments make the maintenance of chronic conditions more difficult. This is especially true for those who lack insurance (Durant et al. 2012).

Licensing laws also contribute to the persistence of regional shortages in physicians. Because licensing laws are passed at the state level and state medical boards provide oversight of the practice of medicine, obtaining a license in a new state can be difficult. Physician licensing requirements are largely homogenous across states. Aspiring physicians are required to pass the MCAT, a national exam, and graduate medical education requirements are consistent from state to state. Despite this fact, re-licensure after a move to a new state is onerous. Physicians must go through the application process: submitting transcripts, letters of recommendation, and practice history to the state board before they can begin to practice. The length of time varies between states, but the California medical board recommends that applicants allow 6 months for their application process (Medical Board of California 2023). Likewise, the AMA warns applicants that although the process can take as little as two months, delays are likely due to the necessary investigation of credentials and past practices (American Medical Association 2023). Thirty-eight states have implemented the Interstate Medical Licensure Compact (IMLC), which makes it easier for physicians moving between member states to transfer their license (Ghosh and Deyo 2022). According to the IMLC the compact reduces the time to obtain a medical license in another state to a few days (Interstate Medical Licensure Compact 2023). The IMLC reduces the cost associated with gaining additional licenses in new states, but the process still requires licensing fees and an IMLC application fee. For those seeking to redesignate their home state, they must already hold an active license, and have a previous relationship with that state, through either practice or residency. As a result, licensing helps maintain regional shortages by reducing geographic mobility.

At the population level, physician licensing may harm patients by reducing access to care, but in theory it can still improve the quality of services for the patients that are able to receive care if it prevents incompetent and unethical people from practicing medicine. However, in practice, most studies find that occupational licensing is not effective at improving quality (Carroll and Gaston 1983; Deyo 2017; Farronato et al. 2020; Thornton and Timmons 2013). During an era where advances in information technology have made it much easier to determine the quality of a service provider, the case for occupational licensing to ensure service quality is even weaker.

Specific arguments also have been made that cast doubt on why licensing may not improve the quality of care that patients receive from physicians. First, licensing may have a small positive effect on quality, but over the long run, the reduction in competition reduces the overall quality of care. Milton Friedman argued that the AMA limiting entry would reduce competition within the practice of medicine, resulting in fewer quality improvements over time. In the typical market with strong competition, competitive pressures are effective in improving quality. Even in imperfect markets where consumers suffer from information asymmetries, competition improves quality of services in the long run. Physician licensing would create both a floor and a ceiling for quality, ensuring that physicians maintained a minimum level of quality, but also discouraging the long-run improvements that dramatically improve quality. Standardizing education, which early licensing laws and the Flexner report both accomplished, prevents the teaching of bad ideas and methods, but also locks in subpar ideas.

Another possibility is that the earliest licensing laws were able to improve quality by professionalizing the field and establishing the first education standards, but there was little subsequent effect. We can see this in the case of midwives. When birthing primarily occurred at home, they were most attended by either untrained women serving as midwives or university-trained physicians. By the late 1800s, states began to require a license to practice midwifery (Anderson et al. 2020). Maternal mortality and infant mortality both immediately fell in states that passed licensing laws, and states with education and exam requirements saw greater quality improvements than states with simpler requirements. However, over time these differences subsided so that differences in education requirements had little impact on health outcomes.

Further evidence supporting the harmful effects of licensing is the case of dentistry, a medical profession whose licensing requirements vary considerably across states. Morris Kleiner and Robert Kudrle compared the dental health of incoming Air Force recruits (2000). They found no evidence that tougher licensing requirements improved dental health. In the case of dentistry, it appears that some minimum licensing standards are enough, any additional increases in education and training requirements are a barrier to entry rather than quality-enhancing. In a similar way, early physician licensing may have been effective in professionalizing the industry, creating standards for education and training that did not previously exist, or was geographically limited. Education standards were central to early licensing laws—and were one of the largest barriers to entry for aspiring physicians (Law and Kim 2005). We have evidence that these mandated higher education standards improved the quality of care that patients received in the early twentieth century. But it is not clear that licensing improves the quality of physicians today, or if licensing is required to attain professionalization. It is conceivable that less burdensome regulatory mechanisms like private certification could achieve the same level of professionalization.

Finally, it is possible that the education and training requirements that are central to licensing laws may not improve quality but may exist solely to convey professionalism. We can certainly see examples of too much education for a number of professions (e.g., barbers). Even the third year of law school that is required for accredited law schools has come under attack as adding little to a lawyer's education and competency (Pagliero 2011, 2013).[5] Shorter education requirements in Europe do not result in substandard care for European patients. Kenneth Arrow, in his early defense of physician licensing, admitted that licensing requirements "merely guarantee training, not continued good performance as medical technology changes" (1963).

8 Self-Interested Behavior by Physicians That Adversely Affects Quality

Physicians are not immune from self-interest. Where state medical boards lack oversight from state legislatures, they are able to behave more anticompetitively. When state legislatures provide a portion of the medical board's operating funds, they have some oversight. In the states where legislatures provided funds, having some measure of oversight, medical boards were less able to restrict entry. But when medical boards are entirely self-funded through licensing fees, they have been able to restrict entry, and we see a lower physician-to-population ratio (Svorny and Toma 1998).

Another way that state boards may facilitate protectionism is through direct lobbying. Board members often benefit from greater legislative

---

[5] As discussed in the first chapter, there are many parallels between the legal and medical professions. In addition to excessive education requirements, each new lawyer must graduate law school and pass the Bar exam to practice. Mario Pagliero (2011) finds evidence that lawyer licensing does not support the quality of services, but instead allows the legal profession to limit entry, decreasing consumer welfare. In fact, when the number of bar exam candidates increases, state bar associations make the exam more difficult (Pagliero 2013). Exam candidates are future competitors for practicing lawyers. Increasing the difficulty of the bar exam when more applicants seek licensure is a clear example of anticompetitive behavior, not consumer protection.

access because they have positions embedded within the government itself. To illustrate, states effectively dictate immigration policy around foreign-trained physicians by virtue of their ability to stipulate that all physicians must complete a residency in either the United States or Canada (despite the fact that Canada recognizes 11 different countries' residencies). Legislative efforts aimed at addressing this discrepancy have repeatedly failed to become law (Graboyes et al. 2022).

While state medical boards work to limit competition, they are designed to provide oversight of physicians to protect consumers. Because, as Arrow admitted, licensing does not guarantee competent practice, professional oversight is an important role if licensing is to be effective. Yet medical boards face the same incentives to protect physicians—their friends and colleagues—instead of patients. It should be stressed that these are common human pressures that we all face, but nevertheless they must be considered.

Medical boards are notorious for lax enforcement and discipline for physician malpractice, despite rhetoric to the contrary. We see a wide variation in disciplinary actions between states, which physicians blame on inconsistent enforcement. To show just how widespread this issue is, let's consider the outlier physicians. In 2019, 8633 physicians had five or more malpractice payment reports. Not all of these physicians are negligent, but this number of payments should be a good sign of substandard care. Over three quarters of these physicians did not have a single disciplinary action taken against them by their state medical board. Medicine is difficult and complaints can result from bad luck or overly litigious patients, but sanctioning just under one quarter of these repeat offenders is too low to suggest that medical boards are providing adequate oversight. When just 2 percent of physicians cause over half of all complaints, catching these physicians should be easy and a priority. There are also problems with malpractice insurance. Other research finds evidence that malpractice insurance premiums vary for reasons completely unrelated to negligence or medical errors, which casts doubts on the ability of premiums to accurately price risk (Tabarrok and Agan 2006).

Another example where state medical boards fail to provide oversight that would help patients is the continuing practice of extended duration shifts for residents. Extended duration is a euphemism for a shift of 24 hours or greater. Current regulations cap residents' hours at 80 hours per week, double the typical work week. According to ACGME guidelines, residents can work a total of 9 extended duration shifts per month.

Furthermore, these limits are more honored in the breach than the observance. Almost 90 percent of residents worked past their consecutive hour limits and admitted lying about the breach (Arora et al. 2008).

Working extended shifts represents more than simply a difficult working environment for residents. It is well-established that these marathon shifts result in unnecessary errors, causing patient harm. When physicians work extended duration shifts, patients suffer 300 percent more fatigue-related adverse events (Barger et al. 2006). Residents admitted to researchers about nodding off on the job—even during surgery. The adverse effects of working more than 24 hours straight are like providing care with a blood-alcohol level of 0.10, which is a crime. Yet, the ACGME considers extended duration shifts "the cornerstone of American post-graduate medical education."

9   How More Market-Oriented Reforms/Regulations Could Help

We have argued that occupational licensing of physicians raises the price and limits the availability of medical services without having much of a long-term effect on the quality of medical service. Self-reform of occupational licensing is unlikely given that physicians have a vested interest to maintain occupational licensing. Thus, is it possible that market-oriented reforms could protect patients while reducing medical costs and increasing the availability of medical services? We argue that not only is it possible, but that we have several options for reform. We offer four options for reform and rank them in order of potential impact beginning with more modest reforms.

Separate Credentialing from Scope of Practice Reforms

Given the previously documented downsides of licensing, the United States almost certainly micromanages the tasks that specific healthcare professionals can perform. Consolidating existing licenses and relying more on title protection rather than scope of practice will likely benefit both American patients as well as the many health industry workers who would be able to provide more highly valuable services as a result of this greater flexibility.

An alternate approach would be to continue the scope of practice movement in the United States. Healthcare professionals with less training than physicians have historically been required to practice with some level of physician oversight. This oversight often involved a signed collaborative practice agreement, which stipulated the relationship between the care provider and the physician. These professionals include advanced practice registered nurses (APRNs) and physician assistants (PAs). APRNs and PAs can practice in a variety of settings, but they most frequently offer primary care and can be a valuable resource to expand patient access to primary care.

Granting full practice authority to APRNs and PAs would allow each professional to practice with greater independence and not be tethered to physicians. APRNs and PAs would be able to practice without a collaboration practice agreement with a physician. This change does not allow these other healthcare professionals to perform additional tasks that they are not trained to perform. In essence, they would be able to perform the same tasks, just now without unnecessary bureaucracy. The current level of oversight is less than compelling, so this reform would not be a radical departure. In some states, APRNs and PAs must be "supervised" by an on-site physician or be located within so many miles for regular visits. In other states, physicians provide token oversight, simply reviewing a portion of patient charts after the care is provided.

Research consistently finds that when used appropriately, full practice authority does not put patients at risk. They have the same health outcomes, and greater access to primary care. Nurse practitioners are more likely to locate in rural areas and HPSAs, providing a source of primary care for patients who previously lacked convenient access. In practice, allowing APRNs and PAs to practice without collaborative practice agreements with physicians is a relatively minor change, but can have a substantial impact.

Additionally, we can expand the practice authority for other healthcare professionals, like pharmacists. Pharmacists are trained extensively in pharmacology, yet just a handful of states grant them prescriptive authority. In 2018, Idaho began allowing pharmacists to prescribe limited drugs and medical devices for minor illnesses and emergency care (Shakya et al. 2022). The Montana legislature passed a similar reform in 2023 (MT SB0112). In rural areas where patients face long drives to emergency care, allowing pharmacists to prescribe medications in emergencies will have a positive effect on patient outcomes.

Shortened Graduate Medical Education

Graduate medical education takes a different form in the United States and Canada than in the rest of the world. Students are required to go through 4 years of undergraduate study, where a bachelor's degree in medicine is not offered, 4 years of medical school, and typically 3 years of residency. The cost of this education can be prohibitive for many aspiring physicians, the average student loan debt for physicians is around $200,000. Instead of 8 years of schooling, European countries offer a 6-year combined medical degree, replacing the undergraduate degree. European countries have more physicians per capita than the United States, and there are no noticeable differences in quality despite the differences in education programs.

Moving to a European-style combined undergraduate medical school degree would simplify physician education. Currently, there are no requirements for applicants' undergraduate degrees. Often, aspiring physicians major in humanities, not something related to medicine. Even when they major in biology or something similar, their coursework is not counted toward their graduate requirements. Undergraduate education serves as an expensive signal of quality to be used in medical school applications, a waste of both time and money, instead of providing actual training. Furthermore, a large percentage of applicants for medical school are turned away, rendering their investment a waste.

A combined undergraduate medical school degree solves these problems. By combining medical education into a single degree, we can ensure each course will prepare students for practice as a physician. Under this reform, aspiring physicians spend four years completing unrelated courses and extracurricular activities to improve their application for graduate medical school. Students can expect to save between $50,000 and $100,000—no small sum. Instead of relying on the application process for medical school as the quality filtering mechanism, programs can rely on grades and comprehensive exams.

While at first glance this may seem like a drastic change to medical education, in practice it will retain many of the characteristics of our current system. We would replace the first four years of education in any subject with two years of education focused on medicine. In practice, most physicians would end up with more medical education, not less. Yet, they would spend less time in school with a less risky and more straightforward process. With less student debt, more physicians will be willing to offer primary care, instead of specializing in more lucrative specialties.

Although 6-year medical degrees have a great deal of intuitive appeal, transitioning away from the current system is easier said than done. Even under the current system, large numbers of qualified medical school applicants are turned away each year due to insufficient enrollment capacity at US universities (AAMC 2023). In part, this is a legacy of the medical school enrollment moratorium of 1980–2005 (Orr 2023). The fierce competition among existing bachelor's degree holders has made it difficult for schools to justify expanding enrollment among those currently possessing only a high school diploma. Despite this headwind, philanthropic efforts have successfully encouraged a few schools to establish 6-year bundled BA-MD programs in recent years.[6]

Simplifying Primary Care License

A physician needs a wide base of knowledge and experience to competently diagnose patients. However, the current licensing standards and graduate medical education requirements may require a much larger base of knowledge than necessary in many cases. Currently, all physicians receive the license to practice medicine, without any limit to areas that they received training. It is other regulations that limit them to their specialty area. Paul Feldstein proposed a specific purpose license, where physicians are trained only in the essential areas for their practice (Feldstein and Melnick 2007).

Outside of general practice, any specialty in medicine would require its own credential to practice, complete with specific education, training, and exam. By limiting education to those who need it, it would allow us to shorten medical education and residencies by removing only what is not necessary for practice. In this way, medical licensing would become task-based instead of profession based. The ultimate goal would be to ensure that the supply of physicians, and their chosen specialty, is controlled by their expected wages, not by the number of residency slots.

In practice, this reform would retain most of the current structure of medical education and oversight. It would not alter the structure

---

[6] See for example this program at Penn State College of Medicine: https://med.psu.edu/md/accelerated/family-medicine.

or authority of state medical boards. It would shorten graduate education and residencies for some physicians who are seeking the simple primary care license. We could allow practicing physicians to obtain credentials in specialties—something that would simplify moving between specialties. There is already some precedence for this type of regulation. Although current medical licensing is profession-based, hospital privileges are focused on the tasks that physicians are qualified to perform. This reform would be a movement in that direction rather than a radical departure.

Simplifying the physician license would help lower the cost of obtaining a license, potentially removing a year. Additionally, the shorter time spent in education would allow students to begin practicing more quickly. It also would encourage more students to enter primary care, because of the shorter education time. If a shortage in a specialty arises, any physician can choose to undergo additional training in just that area, allowing them to enter that specialty more quickly.

A reform that removes required education must be properly designed to avoid sacrificing patient health. Removing too many of the current required topics would leave patients at risk of relying on physicians who are unable to recognize and diagnose certain ailments. Introducing the role of assistant physicians (not to be confused with physician assistants) offers a pragmatic pathway to achieving this (Singer 2023). The medical residency bottleneck poses a significant challenge to the US healthcare system, leaving many qualified medical school graduates in a state of limbo, unable to fully utilize their skills and training. Assistant physicians, being medical school graduates who haven't secured residency programs, can provide essential primary care services, especially in underserved areas, under the guidance of licensed physicians. This not only addresses the immediate need for more primary care providers but also ensures that the skills and knowledge of these graduates are not wasted. Furthermore, by allowing these graduates to practice as assistant physicians, we can bridge the gap between the increasing number of medical school graduates and the limited number of available residency positions, effectively alleviating the strain on the healthcare system and ensuring that communities receive the care they need.

Replace Licensing with Certification

Our final recommendation for reform may be perceived as a more radical reform: removing medical licensing and substituting this regulation with certification. Rather than making it a crime for unlicensed individuals to practice "medicine," certification would protect title and not result in the same restrictions on the market. Only those who completed the state-mandated requirements would be able to refer to themselves as "physicians." State medical boards would still exist to provide oversight to ensure that non-credentialed physicians could not falsely use the title. States could choose to leave the current entry requirements in place for certification.

Certification would remove the information asymmetry between physicians and patients that licensing is designed to solve. Currently, only those who have met the licensing standards can practice medicine. Under certification, only those who meet the standards can use the title (Friedman 1962). Patients receive the same signal of skill level. State medical boards have proven themselves to be ardent and skillful defenders of their profession from encroachment by non-physicians, so we should expect them to be able to continue it against non-certified medical providers. We currently rely on other methods to ensure quality besides licensing, like hospital privileges and malpractice insurance, which would continue to protect patients.

It might be fair to wonder, will we experience a resurgence of snake oil salesmen of the past? Unlike the past, we now have professional associations and state medical boards, as well as a much more mature healthcare system and vastly improved information technology to closely monitor the performance of service providers. In significant portions of the health system, furthermore, malpractice litigation renders many of these certifications effectively mandatory. Instead of allowing anyone without training to provide the care currently provided by a physician, in practice, we would see a greater reliance on other health professionals (Svorny 2008). Moving to certification would also eliminate many of the barriers on tasks related to the practice of medicine–there would no longer be a monopoly in the market on the practice of medicine.

10 Technology as Further Market Disruption

Artificial Intelligence (AI) and Large Language Models (LLMs) are still in their early stages, but they have the potential to disrupt the practice of medicine for the better. They are trained using massive datasets, which enables them to recognize, translate, predict, or generate text. In practice, much of the diagnostic process consists of identifying symptoms and using a decision tree to determine the cause. AI and LLMs seem well-positioned to handle this type of analysis. For instance, ChatGPT, an LLM, was able to earn a passing score on the NBME-Free-Step-1 (Gilson et al. 2023).

Nevertheless, AI and LLMs will not render physicians obsolete, as some fear. Their skills will be necessary to guide the AI or LLM through the diagnostic process and they will still be essential for treatment. These technological advancements provide an avenue for increased productivity, complementing physicians' skillset. Some argue that the increase in spending on medical care is a result of Baumol's cost disease, where services are unable to reap the productivity gains of technological advancements (Helland and Tabarrok 2019). But these advancements do have the potential to complement physicians, thereby increasing productivity.

11 Conclusion

Patients continue to face difficulties accessing healthcare. Thanks to an artificial constraint on the number of physicians—due to our deliberately chosen regulatory policy—large swaths of the country live in areas without adequate access to healthcare and their health suffers from it. As a result, patients are forced to drive long distances, and suffer through long wait times. Care is expensive, inconvenient, and too often, rushed. For decades, the political debate has focused on who pays for healthcare. More recently, the focus has shifted to equity. But ignored in the changing political fashions are the supply restrictions that we needlessly impose on ourselves.

The physician shortage is nothing new and will continue to grow absent a conscious policy change designed to reverse it. This is a self-inflicted wound, not a law of nature. We have one of the lowest physician-to-population ratios in the developed world, despite having the highest wages for physicians. A major culprit is medical licensing laws, which by design limit entry into the medical profession. Fearing an oversupply of physicians, physician groups lobbied to limit residency spots from the 1980s through the 2000s, something necessary to obtain a license. They believed too many physicians practicing would hurt their pocketbooks. Instead, their incorrect forecasts and deliberate steps to constrain supply created an artificial scarcity, and patients suffered as a result.

Although early licensing laws may have helped patients by professionalizing medicine and providing valuable information about physician quality, the current regulatory environment is harming patients by limiting access to care and increasing costs. Supporters argue that medical boards are valuable because of their ability to provide oversight over practicing physicians, a claim which falls apart upon further inspection as the worst physicians are rarely disciplined. In theory, licensing can ensure quality and protect patients; in practice, licensing causes shortages and provides lax oversight once physicians make it through the gauntlet and obtain a license.

There is no easy solution. Layers of overlapping regulatory bodies and professional groups set standards and oversee medicine. Additionally, the practice of medicine is difficult and requires highly skilled and competent practitioners, which has to be remembered when considering any reform. Nevertheless, we provide a menu of reforms for policymakers to consider. Granting professionals like NPs and PAs full practice authority should be an uncontroversial reform, leaving current institutions intact but having an immediate impact. Reforms to physician licensing, like shortening medical education to a combined 6-year program of study or simplifying the requirements for a primary care license would face stiffer resistance but would expand the supply of physicians. An even more impactful reform would be replacing the licensing requirement for physicians with certification—further increasing the supply of physicians and improving access to healthcare in the United States.

The United States would not be alone if it were to move forward with our suggested reforms. Countries like Sweden have a much less restrictive regulatory structure in medicine without a degradation in safety. Given the projections of ever-increasing demand for healthcare, it is critical to make sure that US patients have access to a sufficient supply of providers. Focusing on access to insurance will not address the structural problems in the delivery of healthcare in the United States. We need more providers and scaling back existing regulation seems to be the right prescription to fix the problem.

REFERENCES

AAMC. 2023. Medical Student Education: Debt, Costs, and Loan Repayment Fact Card for the Class of 2022. *Report.* https://store.aamc.org/downloadable/download/sample/sample_id/575/.

American Medical Association. 2023. Navigating State Medical Licensure. Navigating State Medical Licensure American Medical Association. https://www.ama-assn.org/medical-residents/transition-resident-attending/navigating-state-medical-licensure.

Anderson, D. Mark, Ryan Brown, Kerwin Kofi Charles, and Daniel I. Rees. 2020. Occupational Licensing and Maternal Health: Evidence from Early Midwifery Laws. *Journal of Political Economy* 128 (11): 4337–4383.

Arora, Vineet M., Diane B. Wayne, R. Andy Anderson, Aashish Didwania, and Holly J. Humphrey. 2008. Participation in and Perceptions of Unprofessional Behaviors Among Incoming Internal Medicine Interns. *JAMA* 300 (10): 1132–1134.

Arrow, Kenneth J. 1963. Uncertainty and the Welfare Economics of Medical Care. *The American Economic Review* 53 (5): 941–973.

Avi-Yonah, Shera. 2023. Medicine Without Doctors? State Laws Are Changing Who Treats Patients. *Washington Post*, August 20.

Bae, K., and E. Timmons. 2022. Do Restrictions on Healthcare Profession Scope of Practice Help or Harm US Patients? In *Grease or Grit: International Case Studies of Occupational Licensing and its Effects on Efficiency and Quality*, ed. M.M. Kleiner and M. Koumenta, 97–122. Kalamazoo, MI: W.E. Upjohn Institute for Employment Research.

Barger, Laura K., Najib T. Ayas, Brian E. Cade, John W. Cronin, Bernard Rosner, Frank E. Speizer, and Charles A. Czeisler. 2006. Impact of Extended-Duration Shifts on Medical Errors, Adverse Events, and Attentional Failures. *PLoS Medicine* 3 (12): e487.

Basu, Sanjay, Seth A. Berkowitz, Robert L. Phillips, Asaf Bitton, Bruce E. Landon, and Russell S. Phillips. 2019. Association of Primary Care Physician Supply with Population Mortality in the United States, 2005–2015. *JAMA Internal Medicine* 179 (4): 506–514.

Blair, Peter Q., and Bobby W. Chung. 2019. How Much of Barrier to Entry Is Occupational Licensing? *British Journal of Industrial Relations* 57 (4): 919–943.

Büttner, Johannes. 1992. The Origin of Clinical Laboratories. *European Journal of Clinical Chemistry and Clinical Biochemistry* 10: 585–594.

Carpenter, Daniel. 2019. The Social Transformation of American Medicine: The Rise of a Sovereign Profession and the Making of a Vast Industry. *Journal of Health Politics, Policy and Law* 44 (5): 812–817.

CA Statutes. Cal. Bus. & Prof: Code § 2054. https://leginfo.legislature.ca.gov/faces/codes_displaySection.xhtml?lawCode=BPC&sectionNum=2054.

Carroll, Sidney L., and Robert J. Gaston. 1983. Occupational Licensing and the Quality of Service: An Overview. *Law and Human Behavior* 7 (2–3): 139.

Chan Jr, David C., and Yiqun Chen. 2022. *The Productivity of Professions: Evidence from the Emergency Department.* No. w30608. National Bureau of Economic Research.

Deyo, Darwyyn. 2017. Licensing and Product Quality: Evidence Using Yelp Consumer Reviews.

Duffy, John. 1993. *From Humors to Medical Science: A History of American Medicine.* University of Illinois Press.

Durant, Raegan W., Gaurav Parmar, Faisal Shuaib, Anh Le, Todd M. Brown, David L. Roth, Martha Hovater et al. 2012. Awareness and Management of Chronic Disease, Insurance Status, and Health Professional Shortage Areas in the Reasons for Geographic And Racial Differences in Stroke (REGARDS): A Cross-Sectional Study. *BMC Health Services Research* 12 (1): 1–8.

Emmons, Arthur B., and James Lincoln Huntington. 1911. Has the Trained and Supervised Midwife Made Good. In *Transactions of the 2nd Annual Meeting*, 199–217.

Farronato, Chiara, Andrey Fradkin, Bradley Larsen, and Erik Brynjolfsson. 2020. Consumer Protection in an Online World: An Analysis of Occupational Licensing. No. w26601. National Bureau of Economic Research.

Feldstein, Paul J., and Glenn Melnick. 2007. *Health Policy Issues: An Economic Perspective.* Chicago: Health Administration Press.

Friedman, Milton. *Capitalism and Freedom.* University of Chicago Press, 1962.

Ghosh, Sriparna, and Darwyyn Deyo. 2022. Access to Care and Physician Mobility Under the Interstate Medical Licensure Compact.

Gibson, Faith. 2016. The Official Plan to Eliminate the Midwife 1889–1999. In *Wendy McElroy*, ed. Liberating Women, 284–329. Independent Institute.

Gilson, Aidan, Conrad W. Safranek, Thomas Huang, Vimig Socrates, Ling Chi, Richard Andrew Taylor, and David Chartash. 2023. How Does ChatGPT Perform on the United States Medical Licensing Examination? The Implications of Large Language Models for Medical Education and Knowledge Assessment. *JMIR Medical Education* 9 (1): e45312.

Gottlieb, Joshua D. 2021. Who Values Human Capitalists' Human Capital? Healthcare Spending and Physician Earnings. *Census.Gov*, October 8. www.census.gov/library/working-papers/2020/adrm/CES-WP-20-23.html.

Gottlieb, Joshua D., Maria Polyakova, Kevin Rinz, Hugh Shiplett, and Victoria Udalova. 2023. Who Values Human Capitalists' Human Capital? The Earnings and Labor Supply of US Physicians. No. w31469. National Bureau of Economic Research.

Graboyes, Robert, and Murray Feldstein. 2021. For Greater Healthcare Access, License Physicians Like Pilots. Mercatus Center Policy

Brief. https://www.mercatus.org/research/policy-briefs/greater-healthcare-access-license-physicians-pilots.

Graboyes, Robert F. 2022. Arizona Considers Welcome Mat for International Doctors. *InsideSources*, February 9. www.insidesources.com/arizona-considers-welcome-mat-for-international-doctors/.

Helland, Eric, and Alexander T. Tabarrok. 2019. Why Are the Prices so Damn High? The Mercatus Center at George Mason University.

Hermansen, Mikkel. 2019. Occupational Licensing and Job Mobility in the United States. *OECD iLibrary*, December 17. www.oecd-ilibrary.org/economics/occupational-licensing-and-job-mobility-in-the-united-states_4cc19056-en.

Hyman, David A., Jing Liu, and Bernard S. Black. 2022. Should Patients Use Online Reviews to Pick Their Doctors and Hospitals? *Journal of Empirical Legal Studies* 19 (4): 897–935.

ID Statutes 54-5713. https://legislature.idaho.gov/statutesrules/idstat/Title54/T54CH57/SECT54-5713/.

IHS Markit. 2021. The Complexities of Physician Supply and Demand: Projections from 2019 to 2034. American Association of Medical Colleges. https://www.aamc.org/system/files/2020-06/stratcomm-aamc-physician-workforce-projections-june-2020.pdf.

Interstate Medical Licensure Compact. 2023. Information for Physicians. Physician Information | Interstate Medical Licensure Compact. https://www.imlcc.org/information-for-physicians/#:~:text=The%20process%20of%20issuing%20licenses%20in%20IMLC%20Member%20States%20usually,act%20and%20their%20operational%20requirements.

Johnson, David, and Humayun J. Chaudhry. 2012. The History of the Federation of State Medical Boards: Part One—19th Century Origins of FSMB and Modern Medical Regulation. *Journal of Medical Regulation* 98 (1): 20–29.

Kaiser Family Foundation. 2021. Primary Care Health Professional Shortage Areas, September 30. https://www.kff.org/other/state-indicator/primary-care-health-professional-shortage-areas-hpsas/?currentTimeframe=0&sortModel=%7B%22colId%22:%22Location%22,%22sort%22:%22asc%22%7D.

Kett, Joseph F. 1967. American and Canadian medical institutions, 1800–1870. *Journal of the History of Medicine and Allied Sciences* 22 (4): 343–356.

Kleiner, Morris M. 2006. *Licensing Occupations: Ensuring Quality or Restricting Competition?* WE Upjohn Institute.

Kleiner, Morris M. 2015. *Guild-Ridden Labor Markets: The Curious Case of Occupational Licensing.* Upjohn Institute.

Kleiner, Morris M., and Robert T. Kudrle. 2000. Does Regulation Affect Economic Outcomes? The Case of Dentistry. *The Journal of Law and Economics* 43 (2): 547–582.

Law, Marc T., and Sukkoo Kim. 2005. Specialization and Regulation: The Rise of Professionals and the Emergence of Occupational Licensing Regulation. *The Journal of Economic History* 65 (3): 723–756.

Leffler, Keith B. 1978. Physician Licensure: Competition and Monopoly in American Medicine. *The Journal of Law and Economics* 21 (1): 165–186.

"Licensing Health Professionals." *Virginia Department of Health Professions*, 9 January 2023. www.dhp.virginia.gov/.

Leventhal, Justin. 2022. Congress Limits the Number of Doctors. Mercatus Open Health Policy. https://www.openhealthpolicy.com/p/medical-residency-slots-congress.

Ludmerer, Kenneth M. 2014. *Let Me Heal: The Opportunity to Preserve Excellence in American Medicine*. Oxford University Press.

Medical Board of California. Most Asked Questions. FAQs | MBC. https://www.mbc.ca.gov/FAQs/#:~:text=The%20average%20processing%20time%20for,vary%20based%20on%20application%20volume. Accessed 14 June 2023.

MT Statutes. 37-2-101. https://leg.mt.gov/bills/2023/billpdf/SB0112.pdf.

Mullin, Francis J., and John M. Stalnaker. 1951. The Matching Plan for Internship Appointment. *Academic Medicine* 26 (5): 341–345.

OECD. 2023. Health Resources—Data—OECD Data. Organization for Economic Co-operation and Development. https://data.oecd.org/healthres/doctors.htm.

Orr, Robert. 2021. *Unmatched: Repairing the U.S. Medical Residency Pipeline*. Niskanen Center. https://www.niskanencenter.org/wp-content/uploads/2021/09/Unmatched-Repairing-the-US-Residency-Pipeline.pdf.

Orr, Robert. 2023. The Planning of U.S. Physician Shortages. *Niskanen Center*, February 3 www.niskanencenter.org/the-planning-of-u-s-physician-shortages/.

Osborn, Robin, David Squires, Michelle M. Doty, Dana O. Sarnak, and Eric C. Schneider. 2016. In New Survey of Eleven Countries, US Adults Still Struggle with Access to and Affordability of Health Care. *Health Affairs* 35 (12): 2327–2336.

Pagliero, Mario. 2013. The Impact of Potential Labor Supply on Licensing Exam Difficulty. *Labour Economics* 25: 141–152.

Pagliero, Mario. 2011. What Is the Objective of Professional Licensing? Evidence from the US Market for Lawyers. *International Journal of Industrial Organization* 29 (4): 473–483.

Pearse, Warren H. 1983. Is There a Surplus of Obstetrician-Gynecologists? *American Journal of Obstetrics and Gynecology* 147 (2): 133–137.

Peltzman, Sam. 1976. Toward a More General Theory of Regulation. *The Journal of Law and Economics* 19 (2): 211–240.

Phillips, Robert L., George E. Fryer, Frederick M. Chen, Sarah E. Morgan, Larry A. Green, Ernest Valente, and Thomas J. Miyoshi. 2004. The Balanced

Budget Act of 1997 and the Financial Health of Teaching Hospitals. *The Annals of Family Medicine* 2 (1): 71–78.

Plemmons, A., and Timmons, E. 2021. Occupational Licensing: A Barrier to Opportunity and Prosperity. In *Regulation and Economic Opportunity: Blueprints for Reform*, ed. A. Hoffer, T. Nesbit, 116–148. Logan, UT: Center for Growth and Opportunity.

Reuter, James A. 1997. *The Financing of Academic Health Centers: A Chart Book*. Commonwealth Fund.

Roberts, Michael JD. 2009. The Politics of Professionalization: MPs, Medical Men, and the 1858 Medical Act. *Medical History* 53 (1): 37–56.

Shakya, Shishir, Alicia Plemmons, Kihwan Bae, Edward Timmons. 2024. The Pharmacist Will See You Now: Pharmacist Prescriptive Authority and Access to Care. *Contemporary Economic Policy forthcoming*.

Shifman, Holly P., Erika Rasnick, Chiung-Yu Huang, Andrew F. Beck, John Bucuvalas, Jennifer C. Lai, and Sharad I. Wadhwani. 2022. Association of Primary Care Shortage Areas with Adverse Outcomes after Pediatric Liver Transplant. *The Journal of Pediatrics* 246 (2022): 103–109.

Shryock, Richard H. 1956. The influence of the Johns Hopkins University on American Medical Education. *Academic Medicine* 31 (4): 226–235.

Singer, Jeffrey. 2023. One Simple Fix for the Primary Care Shortage: Assistant Physicians. May 18. Stat. https://www.statnews.com/2023/05/18/assistant-physicians-missouri-law/.

Socialsty Relsen. 2022. Ansök Om Legitimation. *Legitimation*. www.legitimation.socialstyrelsen.se/legitimation/. Accessed 11 May 2023.

Starr, Paul. 2017. *The Social Transformation of American Medicine: The Rise of a Sovereign Profession and the Making of a Vast Industry*. Hachette UK.

Svorny, Shirley, and Eugenia Froedge Toma. 1998. Entry Barriers and Medical Board Funding Autonomy. *Public Choice* 97 (1–2): 93–106.

Svorny, Shirley. 2008. "Medical Licensing: An Obstacle to Affordable, Quality Care" Cato Policy Analysis #621, September 7.

Tabarrok, Alexander, and Amanda Agan. 2006. Medical Malpractice Awards, Insurance, and Negligence: Which Are Related?

Table A-23: MCAT and GPA Grid for Applicants and Acceptees to U.S. MD-Granting Medical Schools, 2020–2021 through 2022–2023 (Aggregated). AAMC, October 27, 2022.

Thornton, Robert J., and Edward J. Timmons. 2013. Licensing One of the World's Oldest Professions: Massage. *The Journal of Law and Economics* 56 (2): 371–388.

Wright-Mendoza, Jessie. 2019. The 1910 Report That Disadvantaged Minority Doctors. *JStor Daily*, May 3. https://daily.jstor.org/the-1910-report-that-unintentionally-disadvantaged-minority-doctors/#:~:text=But%20in%20practice%2C%20the%20Flexner,(white%2C%20male)%20membership.

Young, Aaron, Humayun J. Chaudhry, Xiaomei Pei, Katie Arnhart, Michael Dugan, and Scott A. Steingard. 2019. FSMB Census of Licensed Physicians in the United States, 2018. *Journal of Medical Regulation* 105 (2): 7–23.

CHAPTER 4

Balancing Flexibility and Integrity: Reforming Licensing in Accounting and Financial Advising

John M. Barrios

Abstract Reforming occupational licensing in accounting and financial advising is critical to maintaining the integrity and efficiency of our capital markets, which depend on a steady supply of qualified professionals. Current regulations, like the 150-hour rule for CPA licensure and stringent standards in financial advising, have unintentionally tightened labor markets by creating unnecessary barriers to entry, risking the quality and accessibility of essential services. In this chapter, I discuss possible reforms, such as revised educational requirements to make the pathways to CPA certification and financial advising credentials more accessible

---

I am grateful to Jeremy Bartolomeu, Miguel Minutti-Meza, Thomas Wollmann, and John Gallemore for the discussions and comments that facilitated the draft of this piece.

J. M. Barrios (✉)
Yale SOM, New Haven, Conn, USA
e-mail: John.M.Barrios@yale.edu

© The Author(s), under exclusive license to Springer Nature Switzerland AG 2024
C. Winston (ed.), *Reforming Occupational Licensing in the US*,
https://doi.org/10.1007/978-3-031-74349-8_4

while maintaining the profession's high standards. I also discuss how incorporating AI and advanced technologies into professional training can greatly enhance efficiency and ensure that CPAs and financial advisors are well-prepared to meet the demands of today's capital markets.

Keywords Occupational licensing · CPA Reform · Financial advising · AI Integration · Capital markets

1 Introduction

A well-functioning capital market is crucial for economic growth, innovation, and wealth creation. It serves as the cornerstone of economic prosperity, providing a dynamic environment where capital is actively sought and deployed. This, in turn, fosters entrepreneurship, drives investment, and fuels economic expansion. The efficiency and integrity of capital markets are vital for attracting investors, facilitating capital allocation, and enabling corporations to raise funds for strategic initiatives (Beck et al. 2000; Wurgler 2000).

The effective functioning of these markets, however, relies heavily on the expertise and ethical conduct of the professionals in accounting and finance. These professionals play a crucial role in maintaining market integrity by translating complex financial information into actionable insights for investors and decision-makers. This bridging of technical financial details with broader market understanding is essential for the effective functioning of capital markets, fostering an environment where informed decisions about balancing risk and return can be made. Given the complexity of financial information and the potential for misleading data to harm investors, occupational licensing has emerged as a regulatory tool aimed at addressing information asymmetries by ensuring that accounting and financial professionals meet minimum standards of competency, ethics, and professionalism.[1] However, like many well-intentioned public policies, occupational licensing in accounting and finance may not always achieve its desired effects.

Proponents of occupational licensing in financial markets advocate its essential role in protecting investor interests and ensuring the reliability of financial information, thereby contributing to the resilience and efficiency of the financial system. However, this view is not without controversy. Critics argue that while these regulatory measures aim to improve the caliber of finance and accounting professionals, they may inadvertently create barriers to entry, stifle innovation, and reduce competition. Moroever, there is concern that such requirements could lead to a uniformity of skills and perspectives, potentially compromising the dynamic and diverse thinking that is crucial for a vigorous capital market.

The regulatory landscape surrounding finance and accounting professions, while designed to safeguard the interests of investors and maintain the integrity of capital markets, is not immune to the risk of regulatory capture, where industry insiders exert influence over regulatory bodies to shape rules and standards that serve their interests, rather than the broader public interest (Stigler 1971; Peltzman 1976). In this context, regulatory capture manifests as increased licensing requirements that, instead of improving professional quality, may suppress labor supply. These excessive requirements, shaped by the industry's self-interest and influence, create barriers to entry that limit the supply of new professionals into the field.

The impact of such regulatory capture extends beyond mere entry barriers. Increased licensing requirements can lead to a scarcity of licensed professionals, driving up labor costs for firms seeking specialized services (Kleiner 2015).[2] This, in turn, could result in higher prices for financial and accounting services from the resulting concentration, impacting both investors and firms (Allen and Woodland 2010; Pearson and Trompeter 1994; Abramova 2022). The reduced labor supply has the potential

---

[1] In the case of accounting, CPAs with their expertise in financial reporting, auditing, and assurance services instills confidence in investors and stakeholders, contributing to the overall trustworthiness of capital markets (Wallace 1980; Titman and Trueman 1986; Datar et al. 1991; Teoh and Wong 1993; Aobdia et al. 2015). Similarly, in finance, occupational licensing has been promulgated as a mechanism for establishing professionals with the expertise and ethical standards necessary to navigate the complexities of capital markets (Rosen 2013; Nelson 2014).

[2] The wage benefits of occupational licensing, particularly in higher-paying occupations such as accounting, are significantly attributed to reduced competition (Kleiner 2015).

to compromise the efficiency of capital markets and hinder economic growth, as firms face increased costs and investors encounter higher barriers to entry into the capital markets given the potential lower information quality.[3]

The concern of an excessive reduction in the supply is particularly relevant considering the recent widespread decline of accountants. The Bureau of Labor Statistics reports a stark decline of over 300,000 accountants and auditors leaving their jobs in the United States in the past two years, resulting in a 17 percent industry-wide employment decrease. This gap is further exacerbated by the dwindling number of college students opting for accounting as a major (Ellis 2022). The profession's struggle with perceptions of being unglamorous, coupled with the demanding nature of the work and additional educational requirements, has led many potential accounting majors to pursue alternative career paths offering more competitive salaries (Ellis 2022).

A similar downward trend is observable in the finance sector. Data from the Securities and Exchange Commission (SEC) shows a notable decrease in the number of registered broker-dealers. From September 2007 to August 2016, the number fell from 5799 to 4115, a reduction of nearly 30 percent in less than a decade. While this decline can't be solely attributed to the increased compliance costs ushered in by the Dodd-Frank era, particularly in light of the financial crisis that occurred during this period, it's crucial to consider the impact of these escalating costs. The cumulative effect of these trends in both accounting and finance signals a pressing need to reassess and potentially reform the regulatory and educational structures governing these professions.

Moreover, a regulatory environment that enforces stringent licensing without corresponding improvements in professional quality can paradoxically undermine its intended objectives. Such a scenario may lead to increased costs for investors and firms without a commensurate increase in the expertise of professionals. Furthermore, licensing can inadvertently reduce competition among service providers. Established professionals, often grandfathered and exempt from newer, more stringent standards, can gain economic rents—profits exceeding those that would be earned

---

[3] Studies have also shown that high-quality financial advisory can improve a firm's compliance with regulatory standards and the overall quality of financial reporting, thus reducing the risk of costly errors and reputational damage (e.g., DeFond and Zhang 2014).

in a competitive market. As Friedman (1962) noted, licensing laws often disproportionately benefit those already established in the profession, leading to higher service costs and potentially reduced innovation. The recent trends indicating a shortage of professionals in accounting and a decline in registered broker-dealers underscore raise questions about the effectiveness of current licensing regimes and underscore the need for a balanced approach—one that maintains professional quality without hindering the entry of skilled labor.

The licensing situation in the financial markets is further complicated by the potential interplay between inefficiency, rent-seeking, and asymmetric information. While professional associations and regulatory bodies may use licensing to protect service quality and the public, their action can also limit competition, which ultimately harms the public in multiple ways. Balancing the benefits of consumer protection with the costs of limiting market access is a delicate task, which necessitates a nuanced approach to licensing in accounting and finance.

In this chapter, I explore these complexities in detail by first providing a historical overview and current assessment of occupational licensing requirements, focusing on accountants and broker-dealers. I then offer an in-depth analysis of the 150-hour rule in accounting, illustrating how incremental educational requirements can act as barriers to entry, imposing significant costs on firms. Against this background, I propose several reforms for licensing in the accounting and finance sectors that aim at balancing professional standards with market accessibility. For example, in some cases, the proposed reforms are necessary to address potential market failures, while in other cases, deregulation is appropriate. Finally, I reflect on the role of licensing in maintaining well-governed and efficient capital markets.

2 Historical Overview and Current Landscape of Occupational Licensing in Accounting and Finance

Licensing in Accounting

Certified Public Accountants (CPAs) hold a crucial position in the financial ecosystem, primarily tasked with ensuring the accuracy and completeness of companies' financial reports. As highlighted by DeFond and Zhang (2014), understanding how the audit profession can attract and select high-quality CPA candidates is vital. This need has led to the adoption of licensing requirements as a common method to enhance professional quality. These requirements typically include a minimum educational attainment, consisting of 150 semester hours,[4] which is more than the typical 120 hours needed for a bachelor's degree (Kleiner 2015; Leland 1979), along with passing a state CPA exam, requiring at minimum score of 75 out of 99 on each of the 4 parts of the exam, and specific experience prerequisites.[5] The rationale behind these licensing requirements, particularly for CPAs, is partly to safeguard investors who depend on the accuracy of financial information audited by accountants. Since these accountants are neither chosen by nor directly accountable to investors, licensing acts as a protective measure against negative third-party effects arising from incompetent practice.

Despite these potential benefits and increases in the licensing stringencies, research suggests limited evidence of significant improvements in the quality of accounting services, including tax or audit effectiveness (Allen and Woodland 2010; Azzari et al. 2020; Barrios 2022). Accordingly, the restrictiveness of licensing in general has not been without its critics. Notably, Milton Friedman (1962) harshly criticized the concept of licensing standards. Friedman argued that such standards often serve more as a means for existing professionals to restrict market entry and extract economic rents, rather than genuinely improving the quality of practice. This critique highlights the delicate balance between protecting public interest through maintaining professional standards and ensuring open, competitive access to the accounting profession.

(a) *History and Evolution of Licensing Regulation for Accountants*

The roots of CPA regulation trace back to the early twentieth century, marked by concerns about the quality and reliability of financial reporting. The Industrial Revolution's economic transformations necessitated more

---

[4] Within the 150 credit hours, specific coursework in accounting and business is required. This typically includes classes in financial accounting, auditing, taxation, and management accounting, as well as business courses like finance, business law, and information systems.

[5] Passing the CPA exam is acknowledged as a challenging endeavor. The passing rates for first-time CPA candidates are only around 40 percent, indicative of the exam's challenging nature (Espahbodi et al. 2023).

rigorous financial record-keeping, prompting the emergence of professional accountants. However, the lack of standardized practices led to concerns about the accuracy and reliability of financial statements. In the early twentieth century, professional organizations such as the American Institute of Accountants (now the American Institute of Certified Public Accountants or AICPA) were established to address these concerns. These organizations played a crucial role in setting ethical standards and promoting uniform practices within the accounting profession. Finally, the state boards of accountancy emerged to regulate the profession in each state, setting the stage for the development of standardized qualifications for accountants.

In response to the catastrophic impact of the Great Depression in the 1930s, the US government enacted the Securities Act of 1933 and the Securities Exchange Act of 1934, creating the Securities and Exchange Commission (SEC) to regulate securities markets. These acts were instrumental in shaping the regulatory landscape for accounting professionals. The SEC assumed a pivotal role in overseeing financial reporting practices, leading to increased scrutiny of accountants involved in public offerings and securities transactions. To enhance the reliability of financial information, the SEC recognized the importance of establishing a standardized qualification process for accountants.

In response to the SEC's call for standardized qualifications, the American Institute of Accountants, introduced the Uniform CPA Examination in 1934. This marked a significant milestone in the history of occupational licensing for accountants. The CPA exam set a benchmark for competence, ensuring that individuals seeking licensure demonstrated a high level of technical knowledge and proficiency in accounting principles. This national exam aimed to establish a standardized benchmark for assessing the competence of aspiring CPAs across different states.

To oversee the licensing process and regulate the accounting profession at the state level, State Boards of Accountancy were established. Each state developed its own set of requirements for obtaining a CPA license, including education, experience, and successful completion of the CPA exam. This decentralized approach allowed states to adapt licensing requirements to their specific needs while adhering to a common standard.

Having established a national exam, the 1960s and 1970s witnessed a growing consensus among state boards and the AICPA regarding the need for consistent educational requirements. A shift toward a standard

120-credit-hour educational model, equivalent to a bachelor's degree, during this period, reflected the profession's response to the increasing complexity of accounting. Yet, in 1988, responding to the evolving landscape of accounting and business, the AICPA endorsed the 150-hour education requirement. This rule mandated that candidates accumulate a minimum of 150 semester hours of education, which amounts to an additional year beyond a bachelor's degree, to be eligible for CPA licensure, ensuring preparedness for the challenges of modern accounting. This uniformity in the educational requirements by the state boards culminated in 1992 with the development of the Uniform Accountancy Act (UAA) by the AICPA and NASBA. The act was specifically aimed to promote uniformity in CPA licensing. The UAA introduced the concept of experience requirements, emphasizing the importance of practical experience in addition to academic qualifications.

The introduction of the UAA and experience requirements introduced the concept of a two-tier system, where candidates first become certified as CPAs by passing the exam and then fulfill experience requirements for licensure. However, some jurisdictions retained a one-tier system, requiring candidates to fulfill both exam and experience requirements simultaneously. Concurrently, state boards and the AICPA formalized ethical education and evaluation recognizing the importance of ethical conduct. An ethics requirement became a common practice as part of the exam or a separate ethics exam. Finally, changes in standards and technological advancements have led to the requirement to include a focus on maintaining professional competence in the profession. Continuing Professional Education (CPE) became a requirement for license renewal, ensuring CPAs stay current with accounting standards and the technological changes in the industry.

CPA licensing requirements have continued to evolve in response to technological advancements and changes in accounting standards. One example is the move for CPA mobility, where CPAs licensed in one state are able to practice in another state. Recent discussions among policymakers have sought to create more uniform practices to facilitate professional mobility and to serve clients with interstate or international operations, where mobility issues arise.

Licensing Financial Advice

(a) Motivation for Licensing in Financial Advice

The efficient functioning of capital markets is intrinsically tied to the quality of professionals who navigate these intricate financial landscapes. Licensed finance professionals, such as investment bankers, investment advisors, and securities traders, play integral roles in facilitating the flow of capital, advising on investment strategies, and ensuring compliance with regulatory frameworks. In an efficient market, consumers are driven to employ financial professionals when they expect that doing so will maximize their personal welfare. This decision hinges on a fundamental concept: an information imbalance between the consumer and the advisor. In essence, consumers seek financial advice when they believe that the advisor possesses greater knowledge and expertise regarding investments or insurance products, and when the perceived benefits of hiring a financial professional outweigh the perceived costs.

Yet, the critical nature of financial advice sets it apart from other consumer goods or services, where a consumer can rely on credible information that is freely available, such as friends' advice, online reviews, third parties, and the like. An inherent challenge lies in the inability of consumers to accurately assess the quality of financial advice, even after the advice is rendered (Nayyar and Templeton 1994). Unlike tangible products where quality is often immediately apparent, the value of financial advice may not become evident until much later, if at all. For example, a consumer would have to construct a plausible counterfactual outcome without the financial advice to assess whether she received incompetent financial advice. This conundrum highlights the fundamental issue: a consumer who cannot accurately evaluate quality must rely on imperfect cues from the professional to estimate whether the advice provided is of high quality.

Within this dynamic, a principal-agent relationship emerges when a consumer delegates investment or insurance decision-making to a financial advisor (Jensen and Meckling 1976). In an ideal scenario, where the advisor is omniscient and selfless, the outcome is a set of recommendations that maximizes the welfare of the consumer. However, financial advisors, like any agents, are self-interested and have their own preferences. Their aim is to maximize their own welfare, often through generating revenue or perquisites for a given level of input, typically time. This self-serving motivation can lead to recommendations that extract inordinate rents from the consumer, creating a potential conflict of interest.

In such a context, consumers face a daunting challenge. The difficulty lies in assessing the quality of an advisor's recommendation, leaving them vulnerable to the self-serving behavior of the agent. This vulnerability underscores the necessity of effective oversight, contract mechanisms, and advisor-initiated restrictions on self-serving behavior. These mechanisms can collectively be viewed as "bonding" mechanisms, minimizing the agency costs or potential losses consumers incur when they delegate decision-making to financial advisors.

The existence of asymmetric information—the financial advisor knows more about his or her competence than the consumer knows—motivates the case for regulation. Regulation is therefore seen as a critical component of the financial advisory landscape, serving to decrease the monitoring costs for consumers or to increase the bonding costs for financial advisors, particularly when they act imprudently. For example, the SEC employs inspectors to assess the quality of advisor services and impose penalties when advice is excessively self-serving. This type of regulatory oversight is viewed as essential, given consumers (specifically retail investors) typically lack the knowledge and resources to provide adequate oversight themselves. Overall, given this context, licensure is seen as a commitment to upholding industry standards, safeguarding investor interests, and fostering the stability of capital markets (Roychowdhury and Srinivasan 2019).

(b) ***History and State of Licensing Regulation for Financial Advisors, Investment Bankers, and Stockbrokers/Securities Traders***

The enactment of the Securities Act of 1933 and the Securities Exchange Act of 1934, created the SEC to oversee the securities markets, and laid the groundwork for future developments in financial oversight. The Investment Advisers Act of 1940 further expanded the scope of the 34 act, introducing fiduciary responsibility for investment advisors, emphasizing their duty to act in the best interests of their clients. While this legislation did not explicitly introduce licensing requirements, it was instrumental in setting the stage for more sophisticated regulatory mechanisms. As financial markets evolved over the years, additional oversight tools, such as the Series 65 exam and the Dodd-Frank Act, were implemented to ensure advisor competency and prioritize client interests.

Broker-dealers, defined in the Exchange Act as entities engaged in effecting transactions in securities for others or trading on their own accounts, are subject to comprehensive oversight by federal and state entities, as well as self-regulatory organizations (SROs). Registration with the SEC, a key component of this regulatory framework, requires detailed disclosures about the broker-dealer's operations, ownership, and legal history. Additionally, membership in SROs like the Financial Industry Regulatory Authority (FINRA) imposes further rules covering various aspects of their securities business.

Crucial to broker-dealer regulation are the financial responsibility and customer protection rules. The Net Capital Rule, established in 1975, requires broker-dealers to maintain a specific liquid asset-to-liability ratio. According to SEC guidelines, this means a broker-dealer should have more than one dollar of highly liquid assets for every dollar of liabilities.[6] This ratio is critical because it ensures that if a broker-dealer fails or needs to wind down operations, they have sufficient liquid assets to meet their obligations to customers. An orderly wind down would be necessary in situations where a broker-dealer is unable to continue its business, whether due to financial troubles or regulatory issues. In such scenarios, the liquid assets held would be crucial to meet obligations, thus protecting customers from potential financial losses. The Customer Protection Rule further requires the segregation of a customer's assets from the broker-dealer's business activities. This is essential for safeguarding the investments of customers in the event of the broker-dealer's financial failure. Essentially, this rule ensures that customer securities and funds are not used by the broker-dealer for its own business transactions, thereby increasing the likelihood that these assets will be readily available and can be returned to customers if the broker-dealer becomes insolvent.

Broker-dealers also must comply with conduct requirements based on the antifraud provisions of federal securities laws. This includes ensuring fair dealing, suitability of recommendations, and best execution

---

[6] U.S. Securities and Exchange Commission. (2017). Amendments to financial responsibility rules for broker-dealers. Retrieved from: https://www.sec.gov/about/offices/oia/oia_market/key_rules.pdf.

of customer orders. Specific regulations like SHO and M govern circumstances such as short sales and security distributions, and broker-dealers are tasked with supervising their personnel to ensure adherence to all relevant rules and regulations.[7]

In the investment banking sector, the Glass-Steagall Act of 1933, following the Great Depression, initiated the separation of commercial and investment banking. The subsequent Securities Exchange Act of 1934 established the SEC with the authority to regulate securities exchanges and broker-dealers, indirectly influencing the operations of investment banks and fostering a more regulated financial environment.

The establishment of the SEC and the Maloney Act of 1938 authorized SROs, including the National Association of Securities Dealers (NASD), to regulate the conduct of their members, such as stockbrokers. The NASD, formed in 1956, and its eventual evolution into FINRA in 2007 following a merger with the NYSE's regulatory functions, has been pivotal in overseeing the activities of broker-dealers and administering licensing exams for stockbrokers. Moreover, the SEC's introduction of Regulation Best Interest in 2018 marked a significant advancement, aligning the conduct standards for broker-dealers with those of investment advisors and enhancing the protection of retail customers in the financial markets.

To summarize, the evolution of occupational licensing in accounting and financial advice has been primarily driven by the need to address pervasive information problems, such as discrepancies in financial reporting, lack of transparency in advisory services, and the potential for mismanagement or malpractice. Such concerns led to a series of regulations targeting the enhancement of professional competence and integrity.

---

[7] Regulation SHO, includes several key requirements. Rule 200 focuses on the marking of orders placed with broker-dealers, which must be marked as "long," "short," or "short exempt." Rule 201 is a short sale price test circuit breaker, requiring trading centers to have policies in place to prevent short sales at impermissible prices when a stock experiences a significant price decline. The "locate" requirement under Rule 203(b)(1) and (2) mandates that a broker-dealer must have reasonable grounds to believe that the security to be short sold can be borrowed and delivered on the due date. Finally, Rule 204, the close-out requirement, obligates brokers and dealers to take action to close out failure to deliver positions in short sale transactions, ensuring the actual delivery of securities. Regulation M includes rules that aim to prevent market manipulation by restricting activities around public offerings. They cover aspects such as stabilizing and other activities in connection with an offering, and short selling in connection with a public offering. They focus on preventing activities that could artificially influence the market for the offered security.

These measures were designed not only to ensure the technical proficiency of accountants and financial advisors but also to foster trust in the financial markets by enhancing transparency and ethical standards. Reflecting on this regulatory landscape, two questions emerge. First, have these regulations inadvertently led to negative consequences, such as restricted access to the market or increased operational costs? Secondly, and perhaps more importantly, have they achieved their primary objectives of elevating service quality and fortifying consumer protection?

3 Licensing as a Barrier to Entry

The implementation of licensing requirements in the fields of accounting and finance, while aimed at protecting consumers, often leads to unintended consequences that go beyond safeguarding public interest. These regulations, as Barrios (2022) points out, can either inadvertently or deliberately limit the number of professionals entering the field. While such requirements are designed to maintain a high standard of service, they often end up excluding a wide array of potentially capable professionals. This exclusion manifests in various forms, such as the prohibitive costs associated with education and certification, as well as the significant time investment required to obtain the necessary credentials. Consequently, many skilled individuals may be deterred from pursuing a career in accounting or finance, opting instead for alternative careers or non-licensed roles within the financial sector. This shift can lead to a notable reduction in the overall supply of qualified professionals available in the market. This reduction in the supply of qualified professionals who are responsible for protecting consumers compromises the initial effectiveness of the regulation.

A prime example of how licensing requirements can restrict supply without clear evidence of enhancing quality is the 150-hour rule in accounting. This rule, which requires CPA candidates to complete 150 hours of post-secondary education—a significant increase from the traditional 120-hour that a bachelor's degree requires—has been a subject of debate. Critics of this rule argue that the additional educational requirements impose a considerable financial and time burden on aspiring accountants, potentially deterring talented individuals who might not have the resources or the inclination to commit to such an extended period of study. Furthermore, there is an ongoing debate about whether this increased educational requirement translates into tangible improvements in the quality of accounting services or audit accuracy. The introduction of the 150-hour rule thus serves as a case study in examining the effectiveness of licensing restrictions in accounting and whether these measures genuinely contribute to enhancing professional standards or merely serve as barriers to entry, limiting the supply of professionals without commensurate improvements in service quality.

(i) *Assessing the Case of the 150-Hour Rule in Accounting*

In addition to passing a four-part exam, CPA candidates must meet specific educational requirements. Historically, the minimum educational requirement for CPA licensure was 120 semester hours of college coursework, usually completed in four years. Approximately four decades ago, the accounting profession began contemplating a requirement of 150 semester hours of college coursework under the assumption that this change would enhance CPAs training and attract better candidates (Elam 1996).

This push was precipitated by the threat of congressional scrutiny regarding new federal regulation on the accounting profession. Specifically, the savings and loan crisis of the 1980s led to a series of congressional hearings regarding the role of auditors in the crisis. The hearings examined how several prominent public companies, ranging from the Penn Square Bank in Oklahoma to E.S.M. Securities in Florida, failed soon after receiving clean audit opinions (Berg 1988). This led the AICPA in the mid-1980s to implement reforms in the name of "self-regulation" (Madison and Meonske 1991).

One of the main reforms was requiring new AICPA members to have 150-semester hours of college education before receiving membership (Committee 1986). The AICPA, specifically, asserted that the 150-hour requirement was meant to "improve the overall quality of work performed by CPA" and "ensure the quality of future audit" by improving the quality of audit staff and those entering the profession (AICPA 2003). In 1988, at its annual meeting in New York City, 84 percent of the AICPA's voting members backed the proposal, effective for the year 2000. While the AICPA required the rule, the state boards of accountancy had to adopt it for it to be legally required for licensure. Florida had added this requirement in 1983, and every other state followed over the next few decades,

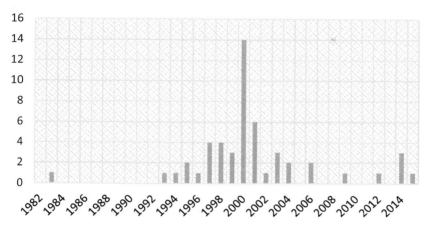

Fig. 1 States adopting the 150-hour rule

as seen in Fig. 1. By 2016, all 54 US jurisdictions mandated a 150-hours education in order to obtain the CPA licensure.

Despite its intention to enhance the human capital of the accounting profession, the implementation of the 150-hour rule has revealed various inconsistencies in achieving its stated goal of increasing CPA quality. For instance, even before the rule's adoption, most jurisdictions required a minimum number of coursework hours in business and accounting.[8] Most states did not change these requirements with the adoption of the rule. This flexibility was granted to allow four-year colleges, which do not have the authority to grant master's degrees, the ability to offer programs that could meet the rule's requirement (Jacob and Murray 2006).[9] Consequently, CPA candidates could fulfill the additional education hours through various means, such as graduate degree courses (like an MBA with an accounting focus or a master's in accounting), a second major at the undergraduate level, or nondegree programs. This wording of the rule, designed to offer programmatic flexibility to colleges and

---

[8] The AICPA pushed for the extra 30 credit hours to be composed of more liberal-arts and general-business courses, rather than pure accounting ones (Collins 1989).

[9] The political economy of the rule can be seen in Oklahoma, where the original bill that required graduate courses to fulfill the rule was not passed after lobbying by four-year universities. The bill eventually passed when the wording was changed to allow 30 additional hours of higher-level education.

universities, has been criticized for potentially allowing CPA candidates to be licensed without any increase in business and accounting-specific coursework.

This array of options for fulfilling the rule's requirements raises questions about its effectiveness in both screening and developing human capital. Specifically, the temporal aspect of the rule—approximately an additional year to complete educational requirements—could result in adverse selection. High-ability candidates, facing a higher opportunity cost of time, might opt for alternative careers (Akerlof 1970). In essence, if the rule's primary effect is to require high-quality candidates to forgo a year of paid work, and these individuals have higher earning potential, the rule could be disproportionately costly for them. This, in turn, might lead to a decrease in the average quality of CPAs, particularly impacting marginalized groups in society.

Early academic studies examining the rule's impact primarily focused on the number of CPA exam candidates. These studies overwhelmingly documented a reduction in the number of exam takers (Boone and Coe 2002; Raghunandan et al. 2003; Allen and Woodland 2006; Jacob and Murray 2006; Briggs and He 2012). Proponents of the rule interpreted these decreases as evidence of its effectiveness in weeding out lower-ability candidates. However, as Barrios (2022) pointed out, a mere reduction in the overall numbers of exam takers is insufficient to distinguish between whether the quality of candidates has improved, or high-ability candidates have opted for alternative careers.

Understanding the profile of candidates who are no longer sitting for the exam is crucial. For example, a decrease in the number of lower-ability candidates does not necessarily equate to an increase in overall quality, as these individuals would likely have failed the exam and would not have entered the CPA labor market even without the rule. Conversely, a reduction in higher-ability candidates suggests a deterioration in quality because these individuals would otherwise have become CPAs. Focusing on the high-ability group, which passes all the exam sections in one sitting, Barrios finds that the number of high-quality test takers fell 10 percent after the rule's implementation.

Figure 2 illustrates the similar decrease in the number of both high-ability and low-ability candidates after the rule's enactment over time. The reduction in the number of low-ability candidates is not necessarily related to an increase in the quality of CPAs in the labor market because those individuals would have failed the exam, even absent the rule, and would not have entered the CPA labor market. The reductions in the high-ability candidates are likely explained by their self-selection to pursue an alternative career.

Given the observed decline of both high- and low-ability CPA exam takers, Barrios evaluated the rule's impact on CPA quality by conducting an analysis of the individual labor market outcomes of CPAs, including the time to promotion and tenure at the firm where they are employed. Despite those metrics being plausible indicators of the quality of individual CPAs, thus increasing the robustness of the tests, Barrios's findings did not show any significant improvement in career outcomes attributable to the rule; that is, there was no notable difference in the time it took CPAs to be promoted that could be attributed to the rule. This finding is robust to a comparison of a subset of rule-abiding CPA audit partners with their non-rule counterparts. As an additional finding, the tenure of individuals at firms shows no significant variation between those who are subject to the rule and those who are not.

When Barrios examined more direct outcomes claimed by proponents of the rule—such as the rule's alleged ability to increase CPAs' retention

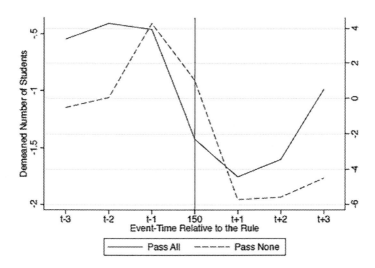

Fig. 2 Demeaned number of candidates taking the CPA exam in event-time relative to the rule year

in public accounting and to enhance their oral and written communication skills (Elam 1996)—he found that for a given timeline, the rule did not significantly influence CPAs' decisions to either exit or remain in public accounting. Barrios also found there is no observable difference in the written communication abilities of CPAs who are or are not subject to the rule.

Further research by Sutherland et al. (2024) delves into the 150-hour rule's impact on minority participation in the accounting profession. Their study finds that a greater educational requirement caused a decline in minority CPA candidates that was 13 percent greater than the decline in non-minority counterparts. This finding indicates that the rule unintentionally increases the challenges faced by less affluent individuals with limited access to financial aid. Finally, this research again suggests that the rule has not led to a significant improvement in CPA quality, thereby questioning its effectiveness in enhancing professional standards.

In a related vein, Abramova (2022) explores the broader implications of this rule on the structure of the audit market. Her study reveals that labor supply shocks triggered by the 150-hour rule increased merger and acquisition activities among audit firms, leading to greater market concentration. The effect was more pronounced in smaller labor markets, which are heavily impacted by the reduction in available labor. The structure of larger labor markets, with a richer supply of accountants, was more resilient to these changes. Abramova's findings suggest that regulatory shifts like the 150-hour rule adversely affect both individual career choices and competition, as in the case of the audit market.

Collectively, these studies paint a compelling picture regarding the 150-hour rule's lack of effectiveness. The absence of marked improvements in career outcomes, professional dedication, and communication abilities among CPAs raises serious doubts about the rule's actual benefits in enhancing the quality and competencies of accounting professionals. This lack of significant evidence supporting the rule's objectives calls into question the overall efficacy of such licensing restrictions in the US labor market.

The situation exemplified by the 150-hour rule highlights a critical need for scholarly and comprehensive cost–benefit analysis to guide implementation of licensing regulations in the financial sector. It underscores the importance of carefully considering not just the intended outcomes but also the potential unintended consequences that such regulatory measures may bring. The insights gained from these studies serve as a reminder that the effects of regulatory decisions cannot simply be assumed. They must be grounded in robust retrospective evidence and a comprehensive understanding of their broader impact on both the profession and the market dynamics.

4 Unlocking Potential: Delicensing Strategies

In the regulatory landscape, the policy choices for change typically fall into one of three categories. The first is inaction, reserved for scenarios where regulation is effectively promoting social welfare. The second option is to undertake reform—a course of action deemed necessary when elements of the existing regulatory framework are adversely impacting social welfare. The third, and often a more radical approach, involves completely dismantling regulations that have outlived its utility and now reduces welfare.

In the context of accounting and finance, I argue that the existing regulatory regime, while well-intentioned in its inception, is presently contributing to unintended consequences, notably a reduction in the labor supply and an unwarranted concentration within the industry. However, I also recognize that some level of regulation is indispensable for addressing the information asymmetries inherent in these professions and ensuring a baseline of professional quality. Thus, in what follows, I propose a series of regulatory reforms, ranging from revising educational requirements to introducing more dynamic, skill-based evaluation methods, which aim to significantly reduce the current costs of regulation on labor supply while still yielding benefits by correcting potential market failures from the unique information challenges faced in the sectors of accounting and financial advising.

(i) *The Case for reforming CPA licensure to improve accountants' services at lower social costs*

Occupational licensing, particularly for accountants, has come under increasing scrutiny in recent years. Critics point out that stringent licensing requirements, while intended to maintain high standards in the profession, may inadvertently create barriers to entry, thereby limiting access to the accounting field. Additionally, growing concerns exist that such licensing could stifle innovation within the accounting industry.

The issue of supply restrictions becomes particularly relevant considering the recent widespread shortage of accountants. The Bureau of Labor Statistics reports a significant decline in the accounting workforce, with over 300,000 accountants and auditors leaving their jobs in the United States in the past two years. This exodus has resulted in a 17 percent industry-wide employment decrease, a gap further exacerbated by the dwindling number of college students opting for accounting as a major (Ellis 2022). The profession's struggle with perceptions of being unglamorous, coupled with the demanding nature of the work, has led many accounting majors to seek other career paths that do not require the additional 30 college credits but offer more competitive compensation (Ellis 2022).

The adoption of the 150-hour rule as analyzed by Barrios (2022) provides evidence that the sharp decline in the accounting workforce has been directly caused by regulation that does not confer benefits to the public. His findings indicate that this regulation leads to a 15 percent decrease in the number of first-time candidates taking the CPA exam, underscoring the significant barrier represented by the additional educational requirement. As noted, the 150-hour rule does not improve the quality of accountants and accounting services.

Importantly, evidence exists that the current national shortage of accountants presents significant challenges for businesses of all sizes. Managers are finding it increasingly difficult to fill accounting vacancies promptly, impacting their ability to maintain essential accounting functions. This shortage is starting to manifest in the financial statements of companies. For instance, large corporations such as Advance Auto Parts have attributed material weaknesses in their internal control over financial reporting to the scarcity of accounting personnel (Maurer 2023).

Empirical studies have begun to assess the impact of this accounting labor shortage systematically. Hann et al. (2023) use the duration of accounting job vacancies as a measure of this shortage, documenting a more than 40 percent increase in vacancy durations over the past decade. They find that firms with prolonged accounting vacancies are more likely to face material internal control weaknesses. This issue is particularly acute for firms with limited financial and labor resources. Furthermore, accounting personnel report lower job satisfaction in environments with extended vacancy periods. These findings collectively paint a picture of the profound implications of an accountant shortage: it can lead to increased risks of internal control deficiencies, employee dissatisfaction, impaired financial reporting quality, diminished firm value, and elevated capital costs. This situation is particularly dire for resource-constrained firms that are less equipped to withstand staffing-related disruptions.

(ii) *Accounting Licensing Reforms*

The significant costs associated with current regulatory frameworks in accounting, coupled with the lack of commensurate benefits, underscore the urgent need for licensing reforms in the accounting profession. These reforms are crucial to address the shortage of accounting talent, which poses a significant economic threat. Stringent licensing requirements, rising educational costs, and declining interest among younger generations have created barriers to entry that limit the supply of new accountants and increase operational costs for firms. Without reform, these trends could exacerbate the shortage, undermining the profession's ability to meet the demands of businesses and markets.

To tackle these challenges, licensing reforms should target the removal of unnecessary barriers while maintaining high standards of quality and ethics. Adjusting educational requirements, like rethinking the 150-hour rule, could make the path to licensure more accessible without sacrificing the quality of accounting education. Additionally, creating alternative pathways to licensure, such as apprenticeship programs or accelerated certification tracks, could help bring in a wider and more diverse pool of candidates. Streamlining and standardizing state-level licensing requirements would also cut down on the complexity and cost of becoming a licensed accountant, making the profession more accessible and promoting mobility across regions. These reforms, which are summarized in Table 1, are essential to addressing the current talent shortage, improving the overall quality of the profession, and ensuring its long-term sustainability.

(a) *Revising the Educational Requirements to Improve Supply*

As discussed earlier in this chapter, the 150-hour rule for CPA licensure, while originally intended to elevate professional standards, has unintentionally contributed to a significant tightening of the accounting labor market. This reduction, as evidenced by the empirical data presented earlier, calls for a thoughtful reevaluation of the CPA licensure pathway.

Table 1 Summary of proposed licensing reforms in accounting

Current regulation	Costs	Reform	Benefits
150-hour rule for CPA licensure	Tightens labor market, high educational cost	Revising educational requirements	Increases CPA candidate pool, maintains quality and integrity
Rigid CPA exam scheduling	Pressures candidates, limits accessibility	Streamlining CPA examination process	Eases candidate burden, attracts diverse cohort, upholds standards
Lack of transparency in CPA licensing	Unclear trends, opaque process	Engagement and transparency in licensing	Efficient resource allocation, adapts to changing profession needs
Generalist CPA license vs certification	Limited specialization	Focus on various certifications	Enhances skill set diversity, meets specific market needs

Building on the analysis we've covered, there's a strong case for reforming these educational requirements to make the profession more accessible, without sacrificing the integrity and quality that the CPA credential represents.

In line with the earlier discussion on making it easier for people to enter the accounting profession and increasing the availability of qualified accountants, there is a strong case to change the educational requirements for CPA eligibility. This rule, while well-intentioned, deters many promising candidates from pursuing the CPA credential. A more practical approach is needed—one that would provide alternative educational paths to meeting the requirements for a CPA.[10] For instance, reverting to

---

[10] Both Minnesota and South Carolina are undertaking legislative efforts to update the CPA educational requirements. In Minnesota, spearheaded by the state's society of CPAs, legislation is proposed to enable individuals who have cleared the CPA exam and amassed 120 credit hours of formal education, coupled with two years of pertinent professional experience, to receive certification. Similarly, in South Carolina, the state's Association of CPAs is championing educational reform. Their draft legislation aims to empower the state Board of Accountancy with the discretion to acknowledge up to thirty hours of educational credit obtained from non-traditional sources, which encompasses a spectrum ranging from unaccredited courses and apprenticeships to certificates, experiential learning, or other alternative educational formats.

requiring a bachelor's degree would be a significant and sensible change. This shift would allow licensing requirements to adapt more flexibly to broader educational trends, with universities determining what constitutes a bachelor's degree, rather than sticking to an arbitrary 120-credit-hour standard. Such a reform would open the doors to a wider pool of CPA candidates, directly addressing the supply issues we've identified.

Additionally, pairing the bachelor's degree with two years of relevant work experience offers a balance between theoretical classroom learning and real-world practical applications. This dual focus acknowledges the multidimensional nature of accounting expertise—one that is cultivated not just in the classroom but also in the dynamics of the workplace. It aligns perfectly with our earlier discussions about the need for dynamic, practical skillsets in the accounting profession. It also ensures that we lower the hurdles to becoming a CPA without compromising the high standards expected of them. This is important because it ensures that the quality and reputation of CPAs are maintained.

A critical benefit of this reform is that it allows for the integration of AI and advanced technology into both the educational and practical training of CPAs. AI has the potential to revolutionize the accounting profession by automating routine tasks, analyzing vast datasets more efficiently, and providing deeper insights through advanced algorithms. By creating a more flexible education system that allows CPAs to tailor their learning paths, we can facilitate smarter investments in education, focusing on areas where technology, like AI, is most applicable. For instance, instead of adhering to a one-size-fits-all approach, future CPAs could select specialized courses or certifications that align with the technological advancements they are most interested in or that are most relevant to their career goals. This flexibility would encourage ongoing learning and adaptation, ensuring that CPAs remain at the forefront of the industry as it continues to evolve.

This proposed reform goes beyond merely adjusting the educational prerequisites for CPAs; it strategically addresses the needs of the accounting job market and the broader industry. By emphasizing a blend of academic learning and practical experience we aim to increase the pool of qualified accountants while upholding the rigorous standards that define the CPA designation. This reform is also about cultivating a more diverse, versatile, and resilient accounting workforce—one that is better equipped to meet the ever-evolving demands of the financial world. It values the varied educational journeys that candidates bring and recognizes the unique perspectives they offer.

(b) *Streamlining the CPA Examination Process*

In concert with revising the educational requirements, another critical aspect of CPA licensure that requires attention is the CPA examination process itself. Recognizing the crucial role that the CPA exam plays in maintaining a quality threshold for the profession, there is a growing consensus that streamlining this process could significantly alleviate the burden on candidates while still upholding the standards that define the accounting profession.

Recent initiatives to provide candidates with more flexibility between exam sittings are a step in the right direction. These changes go beyond mere logistical adjustments; they are a thoughtful response to the evolving needs of exam candidates, many of whom are juggling demanding work schedules, family responsibilities, and other personal commitments. By allowing more time between exam sections, we are not just making the process more manageable—we are making the CPA pathway more accessible to a broader range of candidates. This flexibility acknowledges the diverse circumstances of aspiring CPAs and demonstrates a commitment to inclusivity within the profession.

Building on this momentum, streamlining the CPA Exam could take several forms. One promising approach is to enhance the modularity of the exam, allowing candidates to focus on and prepare for one section at a time without the pressure of an overly compressed timeline. This modular approach aligns well with the proposed shifts toward more flexible educational pathways, creating a more integrated and less intimidating journey to CPA licensure. By breaking down the process into more manageable steps, we can reduce the overwhelming nature of the exam, making it a more approachable challenge rather than a barrier.

Such reforms are not merely about easing the burden on aspiring CPAs; they are about ensuring that the profession continues to attract a diverse and talented pool of candidates. By making the CPA exam process more flexible and candidate-friendly, we can encourage more people to pursue the CPA designation, which in turn helps maintain the high standards and trust that are the hallmarks of the profession. Ultimately, these reforms represent an effort to align the entry points of the accounting profession with the realities of today's candidates, ensuring that the CPA pathway remains rigorous but also accessible and achievable for all who are qualified.

(c) *Engagement and Transparency in Licensing Agencies*

In the quest to reform the CPA licensing requirements, it becomes central to this reform to introduce measures of engagement and transparency. The implementation of a transparent system for reporting the outcomes of the CPA licensing process serves multiple purposes. Firstly, it enables a clear understanding of the licensing trends, success rates, and areas needing improvement. This visibility can lead to a more efficient allocation of resources, reducing the time and financial costs associated with navigating an opaque and unpredictable licensing pathway. For instance, by publicly sharing detailed pass rates and demographic data, stakeholders can identify patterns and challenges unique to certain groups, guiding targeted support and interventions.

While the National Association of State Boards of Accountancy (NASBA) operates to disseminate information to stakeholders, it's evident that there are aspects of the system that appear outdated and in need of modernization. This is particularly apparent in the context of NASBA's cessation of reporting CPA exam pass rates post-pandemic, a move that has sparked discussions about the transparency and responsiveness of the CPA licensing process.

The discontinuation of public reporting of pass rates by NASBA is a significant departure from what has traditionally been a key indicator of the effectiveness and rigor of the CPA examination process. These statistics provided valuable insights into the examination's difficulty and trends over time, serving as a benchmark for educators, candidates, and employers alike. Without this data, stakeholders are left without a crucial tool to assess and adapt to the changing requirements of the profession.

The absence of such reporting can be seen as symptomatic of a larger issue—the need for a more adaptive and forward-looking approach in how NASBA administers the CPA licensing process. In today's fast-paced and ever-changing financial landscape, the accounting profession requires a regulatory body that is not only transparent but also proactive in its engagement with the challenges and opportunities presented by the market. For example, a modernized system under NASBA could include enhanced mechanisms for feedback and continuous improvement, aligning with our earlier discussions on engagement and transparency. This could involve not only reinstating the publication of pass rates but also providing timelier detailed and segmented data, offering deeper insights into the exam's efficacy across different demographics and educational backgrounds.

(d) *A Focus on Voluntary Certification*

Beyond reforming the CPA licensing process, there is a strong case for placing greater emphasis on the role of voluntary certifications in enhancing the caliber of professionals within the accounting and finance sectors. Certifications such as Certified Risk Manager (CRM), Certified Internal Auditor (CIA), Certified Business Valuator (CBV), and Certified Financial Planner (CFP) represent specialized areas of expertise that can significantly augment the skill set of accounting and finance professionals.

These certifications go beyond the broad-based knowledge tested in the CPA exam, delving into specific, often complex, areas of financial management and analysis. For instance, the CRM certification equips professionals with advanced skills in identifying, assessing, and managing risk, which is crucial in today's volatile market environments. Similarly, the CIA designation is focused on the critical field of internal auditing, ensuring professionals are adept at conducting thorough and effective audits within organizations.

The CBV and CFP certifications address other vital areas. While the CBV focuses on business valuation, an essential skill in mergers and acquisitions, corporate restructuring, and investment analysis, the CFP covers aspects of financial planning, offering expertise in wealth management, retirement planning, and personal finance. These certifications, therefore, provide accountants and financial professionals with targeted competencies that are highly valued in the market.

Emphasizing these certifications as part of a professional's career development can significantly enhance the quality of service in the accounting and finance sectors. By encouraging practitioners to acquire these additional credentials, the industry can ensure a workforce that is not only diverse in its skills but also capable of addressing the specific needs of various clients and market scenarios. This approach aligns with the previously discussed themes of continuous professional development and adaptation to market needs.

Moreover, these certifications can serve as a mechanism to differentiate professionals in the marketplace, providing them with a competitive edge and offering employers and clients a clear marker of expertise. They also contribute to raising the overall standard of the profession by requiring ongoing education and adherence to rigorous ethical standards, akin to those upheld by the CPA credential.

Collectively, each of these proposed reforms above aims to reduce the existing costs associated with stringent regulatory measures, like higher educational costs, limited-service availability, and the challenges of keeping pace with the evolving accounting landscape. Importantly, these reforms achieve this without introducing new costs, instead fostering a more dynamic and efficient pathway into the accounting profession. The overall impact is a more robust supply of well-qualified accountants and an enhancement in the quality of accounting services, thereby benefiting the industry and its clients.

(iii) *The Case for Reforming Licensing in Financial Advising to Improve Financial Services at Lower Social Cost*

The current regulatory framework governing broker-dealers and financial advisors is a complex tapestry of rules and standards, presenting significant challenges for both consumers and industry professionals. This complexity stems from the diverse nature of the financial advisory profession, which encompasses various specialties, each governed by its own set of regulations. For instance, while some financial advisors operate under a fiduciary standard, requiring them to act in their clients' best interests, others follow a suitability standard, which only mandates that their recommendations be suitable for the client's financial needs and circumstances. This disparity in standards often leads to confusion among consumers who may struggle to understand the level of care and commitment they can expect from their financial advisors.

The debate over adopting a unified fiduciary standard highlights the industry's divergent interests. Many firms, operating under a suitability standard, oppose stricter fiduciary regulations, fearing reduced flexibility in product recommendations and potential impacts on revenue. This opposition suggests that the current regulatory system may inadvertently prioritize the profit of advisors or firms over the welfare of clients.

Adding to this complexity is the involvement of multiple regulatory bodies, including prominent organizations like the Securities and Exchange Commission (SEC) and the Financial Industry Regulatory Authority (FINRA), alongside state-level entities like insurance regulators. This multi-layered approach can be particularly challenging for financial advisors offering a diverse range of services and products, leading to potential regulatory gaps and inconsistent enforcement. Furthermore, the current system may foster a false sense of security among consumers, who might overly rely on regulatory oversight, thus neglecting their due diligence. Regulations can give the impression that adequate consumer protection is in place, potentially allowing less scrupulous advisors to operate within the legal boundaries but not necessarily in the best interests of their clients.

The tangible impacts of these complexities on the industry are evident. For example, in September 2007, the Securities and Exchange Commission (SEC) had 5799 broker-dealers registered. By August 2016, this number had reduced to 4115, marking a decrease of nearly 30 percent in less than a decade. While not all this decline can be directly attributed to the increased compliance costs in a post-Dodd-Frank world, particularly considering the financial crisis that occurred in the interim, it would be imprudent to disregard the role that escalating compliance costs have played in this reduction. The ever-increasing cost of compliance, a factor that cannot be entirely dismissed even by staunch proponents of free-market principles, has undeniably contributed to the dwindling number of broker-dealers.

This significant reduction in registered broker-dealers highlights the need for comprehensive reform in the licensing and regulation of financial advisors and broker-dealers. This reform should streamline the regulatory process, making it more accessible for consumers and more manageable for advisors. Potential changes could include consolidating regulatory bodies or establishing a universal fiduciary standard applicable across the profession. Simplifying the regulatory landscape would not only enhance consumer protection and confidence but also alleviate the administrative burden on financial professionals. Moving toward a more transparent and straightforward system would better serve the interests of both consumers and ethical financial professionals.

(iv) *Finance Licensing Reforms*

Reforming the licensing and regulatory standards in the financial advisory and broker-dealer sectors is crucial. Such changes could lead to greater clarity for consumers, improved compliance for advisors, and ultimately, a more trustworthy and efficient financial advisory system. The proposed reforms, summarized in Table 2, offer a clear roadmap for reducing operational costs, improving service quality, and facilitating greater accessibility to the profession. By creating a more streamlined and coherent regulatory framework, these changes promise to support the long-term health and integrity of the financial advisory and broker-dealer sectors, ultimately benefiting consumers, professionals, and the broader financial system.

(a) *Revising Standards of Care in Financial Advice*

Financial advising is at a critical juncture, marked by the prevalent use of suitability standards. These standards, originally designed to ensure that financial advisors make recommendations appropriate to their clients' circumstances, have increasingly come under scrutiny. The core issue with suitability standards is their potential to engender conflicts of interest, often leading to increased legal disputes. This situation underscores a pressing need for reform, steering toward the adoption of fiduciary standards.

Fiduciary standards, by their very nature, necessitate that financial advisors act unequivocally in the best interests of their clients. Adopting these standards would represent a fundamental shift in the advisory landscape. The primary advantage of this change is the significant enhancement of client trust. By obligating advisors to prioritize client welfare over their own, fiduciary standards are poised to foster deeper, more enduring client relationships. A fiduciary approach has the potential to considerably minimize legal disputes arising from questionable advisory practices, thereby fostering a more transparent and reliable financial advising environment. This shift is also likely to reduce long-term costs stemming from conflicts of interest, which are a frequent byproduct of the current suitability framework.

Furthermore, this proposed reform addresses the current coexistence of multiple standards of care in financial advising. This multiplicity not

Table 2 Summary of proposed licensing reforms in finance

Current regulation	Costs	Reform	Benefits
Suitability standards	Potential conflicts of interest, legal disputes	Fiduciary standards	Enhanced client trust, reduced conflicts, long-term relationship stability
Multiple standards of care	Regulatory confusion, higher compliance costs	Unified standard of care	Simplified compliance, cost reduction, increased market efficiency
Redundant federal and state oversight	High administrative and compliance costs	Streamlining oversight	Lower operational costs, more competitive service pricing
External regulation	Inefficiencies in monitoring and enforcement	Self-regulation and peer review	Lower operational costs, maintained ethical standards
Manual compliance monitoring	Time-consuming and resource-intensive processes	Technology-driven compliance platforms	Increased efficiency, reduced resource use
Non-standardized professional criteria	Uneven quality standards, higher training costs	Industry-led certification programs	Consistent quality, economies of scale in training
Lack of transparency in advising	Consumer confusion, less competitive market	Transparency and competitive standards	Better informed consumers, competitive pricing, service improvement
Traditional licensing and compliance	Administrative burdens, slow adaptation to change	Tech integration in licensing	Streamlined processes, reduced administrative costs
Limited accessibility of financial advice	High costs of traditional advisory services	FinTech innovations	Wider access, reduced reliance on expensive services, flexible licensing
Traditional risk assessment	Over-reliance on specific professional qualifications	Advanced risk assessment tools	Diversified advisory sector, cost-effective risk management

only creates regulatory confusion but also escalates compliance costs for financial advisors. Implementing a unified fiduciary standard would streamline this regulatory labyrinth. It would eliminate the complexity inherent in navigating disparate standards, thereby lessening the regulatory and financial burden on advisors. The benefits of streamlining extend beyond cost reduction; as it is anticipated to create a more efficient market characterized by clearer and more consistent advisory practices.

In essence, shifting to fiduciary standards is a reformative step that promises multiple benefits. It aligns with the evolving expectations of consumers who increasingly demand greater transparency and accountability from their financial advisors. This reform would not only elevate the level of trust in financial advisory services but also pave the way for a more efficient and ethical market. Such a transition, while challenging, holds the potential to reshape the financial advisory landscape, aligning it more closely with the best interests of clients and the broader market.

(b) *Overhauling Regulatory Oversight*

Similarly in addressing the current challenges within financial advising's regulatory framework, it is crucial to recognize the inefficiencies stemming from the overlap of federal and state oversight. This redundancy not only complicates compliance processes but also increases operational costs. Streamlining these regulations is imperative, aiming to minimize unnecessary expenses and simplify compliance for firms. Such streamlining could lead to more competitive service pricing, ultimately benefiting consumers.

Furthermore, the current regulatory environment lacks a systematic mechanism for inter-jurisdictional coordination (Bhargava 2009; Gallagher 2016; Honigsberg et al. 2022). This gap in communication and tracking is evident in the interactions between entities like FINRA and the SEC, despite informal referral systems and voluntary disclosure practices. Policymakers should consider mandates for federal regulators to systematically track and disclose outcomes related to advisor misconduct referrals. This step would improve transparency and accountability across jurisdictions.

In conjunction with these initiatives, the promotion of self-regulation and peer review within the industry could serve as a cost-effective and responsive approach to maintaining high ethical standards. The current non-standardized professional criteria in financial advising lead to uneven quality standards and higher training costs. By allowing the industry to develop and enforce its own certification programs, these costs can be reduced while maintaining high standards of quality. This strategy, coupled with enhanced inter-agency coordination and the utilization of technology in compliance, can yield a regulatory environment that is both efficient and robust.

In sum, the reform of regulatory oversight in financial advising requires a multifaceted approach. Streamlining overlapping regulations, enhancing coordination and accountability between regulatory bodies, and integrating technology-driven compliance platforms are key to achieving a more efficient and ethical financial advisory landscape. These reforms aim to create a regulatory framework that effectively balances the demands of oversight with the practical needs of the industry, ultimately ensuring the highest standards of service and trust for consumers.

(c) *Transparency and Fostering Technology Integration*

In the process of modernizing the regulatory framework for financial advising, enhancing transparency is as crucial as streamlining compliance monitoring. Traditional compliance methods, while thorough, often result in time-intensive processes that strain both financial institutions and their clients. The integration of technology-driven platforms, particularly blockchain and other FinTech innovations, presents a groundbreaking opportunity to revolutionize this sector. By leveraging these technologies, not only can financial advisory firms significantly boost their compliance efficiency, but they can also offer greater transparency in their services.

For instance, the often-cumbersome processes of customer onboarding and transaction handling, burdened by repetitive Know Your Customer (KYC) requests, can be streamlined through Distributed Ledger Technology. This move not only alleviates inefficiencies but also opens avenues for enhanced transparency in financial transactions. A transparent system, where clients have clear visibility into the processes and standards of service, inherently builds trust and can mitigate the confusion and frustration that often drive clients to seek alternative providers.

The lack of transparency in financial advising, as evidenced in the sector's current state, often leads to consumer confusion, and diminishes market competitiveness. By integrating technology-driven solutions that promote transparency in services and fees, the financial advising industry can foster a more informed consumer base. This informed base, in turn, drives improvements in service quality. With greater transparency comes the potential for more competitive standards, leading to superior services at more reasonable prices.

Furthermore, these technological advancements extend beyond compliance and transparency. They play a pivotal role in reshaping the landscape of financial advice, making it more accessible and reducing the reliance on traditional, cost-intensive advisory models. Blockchain technology, potentially democratizes financial advice by making it more accessible, while simultaneously enabling more adaptable licensing structures. This adaptability is crucial for aligning with the evolving market needs and dynamics of financial services.

In summary, the reform of financial advising through the integration of technology goes beyond enhancing compliance efficiency. It embraces the critical need for transparency in financial services. The future of blockchain, along with other FinTech innovations, lies in creating a more efficient, transparent, and client-centric financial sector. This transformative approach not only caters to the immediate needs of compliance and efficiency but also addresses the broader goal of making financial advice more accessible, competitive, and transparent, thereby reshaping the financial advising landscape for the better.

5 Conclusion

In this chapter, I have sought to navigate the complex landscape of occupational licensing reform in the accounting and financial advising sectors. The proposed framework takes a nuanced approach toward improving occupational licensing, addressing the distinct needs and challenges within each field. In accounting, while regulation is necessary to uphold professional standards, the recommended reforms focus on recalibrating the existing system rather than dismantling it. By revising educational requirements and streamlining the CPA examination process, these reforms aim to make the profession more accessible and adaptable, without compromising the integrity and quality of the CPA designation.

In contrast, the financial advising sector would benefit from selective deregulation, particularly through the transition from suitability to fiduciary standards and the overhaul of regulatory oversight, including the integration of FinTech innovations like blockchain. Such reforms are aimed at reducing administrative burdens, promoting transparency, and enhancing efficiency in the sector, which are increasingly demanded in a rapidly evolving financial landscape.

The successful adoption of these recommendations, however, depends on several factors. In accounting, resistance may arise from those who benefit from the status quo, but the growing recognition of labor shortages and the need to remain competitive in a global market could drive acceptance of these necessary changes. In financial advising, skepticism may come from traditionalists wary of deregulation and technological integration, but the clear benefits of increased efficiency and customer satisfaction are likely to garner support from forward-thinking stakeholders and policymakers.

If these reforms are not adopted, the accounting profession risks continuing to face labor shortages and a potential disconnect with contemporary business practices, while financial advising could struggle with inefficiency and a lack of competitiveness in an increasingly technology-driven market. The failure to reform could hinder the growth and adaptation of these professions, ultimately affecting their ability to serve the evolving needs of businesses and consumers effectively.

In conclusion, the path to reform calls for a collaborative approach among industry stakeholders, educators, consumers, and policymakers. In carefully considering and potentially implementing these reforms, the accounting and financial advising sectors can look forward to a more dynamic, inclusive, and efficient future, ensuring their continued relevance and value in a rapidly changing global economy.

References

Abramova, Inna. 2022. Labor Supply and Accounting Firm Mergers, PhD diss., Massachusetts Institute of Technology.

AICPA. 2003. Background Information on the 150-hour Education Requirement for CPA Certification and Licensure.

Akerlof, G. A. 1970. The Market for Lemons: Quality Uncertainty and the Market Mechanism. *The Quarterly Journal of Economics* 84 (3): 488–500.

Allen, A., and A.M. Woodland. 2006. The 150-Hour Requirement and the Number of CPA Exam Candidates, Pass Rates, and the Number Passing. *Issues in Accounting Education* 21 (3): 173–193.

Allen, A., and A. Woodland. 2010. Education Requirements, Audit Fees, and Audit Quality. *Auditing: A Journal of Practice & Theory* 29 (2): 1–25.

Aobdia, Daniel, Chan-Jane. Lin, and Reining Petacchi. 2015. Capital Market Consequences of Audit Partner Quality. *The Accounting Review* 90 (6): 2143–2176.

Azzari, V., E.W. Mainardes, and F.M. da Costa. 2020. Accounting Services Quality: A Systematic Literature Review and Bibliometric Analysis. *Asian Journal of Accounting Research* 6 (1): 80–94.

Barrios, John M. 2022. Occupational Licensing and Accountant Quality: Evidence from the 150-Hour Rule. *Journal of Accounting Research* 60 (1): 3–43.

Beck, Thorsten, Ross Levine, and Norman Loayza. 2000. Finance and the Sources of Growth. *Journal of Financial Economics* 58 (1–2): 261–300.

Berg, E. N. 1988. C.P.A. Group Votes to Alter Membership Criteria. *The New York Times*.

Bhargava, Nikhil. 2009. Broker-Dealers and Investment Advisers: The Administration's Plans for the Future of Regulation. *Administrative Law Review* 61: 907.

Boone, J., and T. Coe. 2002. The 150-Hour Requirement and Changes in the Supply of Accounting Undergraduates: Evidence from a Quasi-experiment. *Issues in Accounting Education* 17 (3): 253–268.

Briggs, G., and L. He. 2012. The 150 Credit-Hour Requirement and CPA Examination Pass Rates—A Four Year Study. *Accounting Education* 21 (1): 97–108.

Collins, S. 1989. Meeting the New 150-Hour Standard. *Journal of Accountancy* 168 (2): 55–58.

Committee, A. 1986. Restructuring Professional Standards to Achieve Professional Excellence in a Changing Environment. Technical report, AICPA-Report of the Special Committee on Standards of Professional Conduct for Certified Public Accountants, April.

DeFond, M., and J. Zhang. 2014. A review of Archival Auditing Research. *Journal of Accounting and Economics* 58 (2–3): 275–326.

Datar, S.M., G.A. Feltham, and J.S. Hughes. 1991. The Role of Audits and Audit Quality in Valuing New Issues. *Journal of Accounting & Economics* 14: 3–49.

Elam, R. 1996. Is the 150-Hour Requirement Really Progress? *Issues in Accounting Education* 11: 205–206.

Ellis, T. 2022. The Disappearing Act: Why Are Accountants Leaving the Industry? *Journal of Business Studies* 25 (2): 341–356.

Espahbodi, A., L. Espahbodi, R. Espahbodi, R. Walker, and G.T. White. 2023. Determinants of CPA Exam Performance. *Journal of Accounting Education* 64: 100859.

Friedman, M. 1962. *Capitalism and Freedom*. University of Chicago Press.

Gallagher, Daniel M. 2016. US Broker-Dealer Regulation. Reframing *Financial Regulation: Enhancing Stability and Protecting Consumers*, 137–154.

Hann, Rebecca N., Jingwen Yang, and Yue Zheng. 2023. The Price of an Accountant Shortage: Evidence from Job Vacancy Duration and Internal Control Weaknesses.

Honigsberg, C., E. Hu, and R.J. Jackson Jr. 2022. Regulatory Arbitrage and the Persistence of Financial Misconduct. *Stanford Law Review* 74: 737.

Jacob, J., and D. Murray. 2006. Supply-Side Effects of the 150-Hour Educational Requirement for CPA Licensure. *Journal of Regulatory Economics* 30 (2): 159–178.

Jensen, M. C., and Meckling, W. H. 1976. Theory of the Firm: Managerial Behavior, Agency Costs and Ownership Structure. *Journal of Financial Economics* 3 (4): 305–360.

Kleiner, M.M. 2015. Occupational Licensing and Regulation. IZA World of Labor. https://doi.org/10.15185/izawol.188.

Leland, Hayne E. 1979. Quacks, Lemons, and Licensing: A Theory of Minimum Quality Standards. *Journal of Political Economy* 87 (6): 1328–1346.

Madison, Roland, and Norman Meonske. 1991. Education: 150 Semester Hours: The Train Has Not Left the Station. *Woman CPA* 53 (4): 15.

Maurer, M. 2023. The Accountant Shortage Is Showing Up in Financial Statements. *The Wall Street Journal*.

Nayyar, Praveen R., and Patricia L. Templeton. 1994. Seller Beware: Information Asymmetry and the Choice of Generic Competitive Strategies for Service Businesses. *Advances in Services Marketing and Management* 3: 95–126.

Nelson, William Alan II. 2014. Broker-Dealer: A fiduciary by any other name. *Fordham Journal of Corporate & Financial Law* 20: 637.

Pearson, T., and G. Trompeter. 1994. Competition in the Market for Audit Services: The Effect of Supplier Concentration on Audit Fees. *Contemporary Accounting Research* 11 (1): 115–135.

Peltzman, Sam. 1976. Toward a More General Theory of Regulation. *The Journal of Law and Economics* 19 (2): 211–240.

Raghunandan, K., W. Read, and C. Brown. 2003. The 150-Hour Rule: Does It Improve CPA Exam Performance? *Managerial Auditing Journal* 18 (1): 31–38.

Rosen, Kenneth M. 2013. Financial Intermediaries as Principals and Agents. *Wake Forest Law Review* 48: 625.

Roychowdhury, Sugata, and Suraj Srinivasan. 2019. The Role of Gatekeepers in Capital Markets. *Journal of Accounting Research* 57 (2): 295–322.

Stigler, George J. 1917. The Theory of Economic Regulation. *The Bell Journal of Economics and Management Science* 2 (1): 3.

Sutherland, A.G., M. Uckert, and F.W. Vetter. 2024. Occupational Licensing and Minority Participation in Professional Labor Markets. *Journal of Accounting Research* 62 (2): 453–503.

Titman, S., and B. Trueman. 1986. Information Quality and the Valuation of New Issues. *Journal of Accounting & Economics* 8: 159–621.

Teoh, S.H., and T.J. Wong. 1993. Perceived Auditor Quality and the Earnings Response Coefficient. *The Accounting Review* 68: 346–366.

Wallace, W.A. 1980. *The Economic Role of the Audit in Free and Regulated Markets*. Aid to Education Program: Touche Ross & Co.

Wurgler, Jeffrey. 2000. Financial Markets and the Allocation of Capital. *Journal of Financial Economics* 58 (1–2): 187–214.

CHAPTER 5

Conclusions

Clifford Winston

Abstract This chapter summarizes the contents of the book by comparing and contrasting the authors' assessments of the effects of occupational licensing in the legal, medical, and financial professions and their recommendations for reforming occupational licensing in those professions. The authors agree that occupational licensing has imposed significant costs on consumers of the professions' services. However, they vary in their recommendations of how much reform is appropriate for licensing in each profession.

Keywords Occupational licensing · Legal profession · Medical profession · Financial profession

By conducting in-depth analyses of the effects of occupational licensing in the leading professions of law, medicine, and finance, the authors of the preceding chapters have illuminated the full costs of licensing and

---

C. Winston (✉)
Economic Studies Program, Brookings Institution, Washington, DC, USA
e-mail: CWINSTON@brookings.edu

© The Author(s), under exclusive license to Springer Nature Switzerland AG 2024
C. Winston (ed.), *Reforming Occupational Licensing in the US*,
https://doi.org/10.1007/978-3-031-74349-8_5

the potential benefits from constructive reforms for licensing people who work in those professions.

The authors point out that by limiting the supply of lawyers, physicians, accountants, and broker-dealers, licensing has raised the price and restricted access to vital legal, medical, and financial services, especially for less-affluent people and small firms that cannot afford to pay for those services. At the same time, the authors conclude that many of the entry barriers to professional practice in the leading professions have done very little to improve the quality of the services provided and to protect consumers from incompetent and unethical practitioners. Thus, the primary benefit of occupational licensing has been to generate large economic rents to firms and workers in those professions.

Importantly, the broader public may not realize that occupational licensing may be responsible for creating significant costs that reverberate throughout society. Winston argues that the siloing effect of licensing on lawyers, who play a significant role in shaping public policy, may be detrimental to the effectiveness of legal systems and even be responsible for Supreme Court Justices increasingly making decisions based on their ideologies. Norris, Orr, and Timmons argue that licensing has raised the cost of medical care in the United States, thus compromising a primary goal of the federal government to create a healthcare system with lower costs. Finally, Barrios argues that licensing in the financial markets can cause internal control deficiencies, employee dissatisfaction, and impaired financial reporting quality, which diminishes the value of US firms and increases capital costs in the US economy.

As a constructive approach to reforming occupational licensing, the authors argue that consumers of each professional service could benefit if occupational licensing were curtailed and market forces were allowed to play a greater role in ensuring the competence and quality of service providers. However, the authors differ in the extent that they believe that occupational licensing's education and certification requirements should be curtailed.

The cost of acquiring an education at a professional school to work in one of the leading professions accounts for a large share of the cost of occupational licensing because it saddles future practitioners with considerable debts. Accordingly, when those workers enter the workforce, they may be forced to take more lucrative instead of more socially beneficial career paths to repay those debts. In addition, the out-of-pocket and opportunity costs of an education at a professional school may simply discourage some highly qualified people from entering one of the leading professions.

Winston argues that education requirements in the legal profession should be eliminated. Instead, there should be no entry barriers to providers of different types of legal education and the market should be allowed to determine the type of legal education that prospective lawyers should obtain if they want to provide particular legal services and to develop a good reputation among colleagues and consumers. Norris, Orr, and Timmons do not call for eliminating education requirements in the medical profession, but they do suggest that those requirements could be reformed to benefit physicians and patients by reducing their costs and expanding the supply of qualified physicians. For example, a sound medical education could be obtained in a combined undergraduate and medical school 6-year program of study that is similar to programs offered in Europe. Barrios suggests that a credible approach would be to streamline the education requirements in accounting, reducing the 150-hour education requirement to a 120-hour requirement akin to a bachelor's degree, and supplementing it with two years of relevant work experience.

The authors also argue that the entry barriers created by licensing should be reformed. Winston argues that despite their different motivations, the entry barriers to the legal industry are similar to entry barriers to other industries, which deregulation successfully eliminated. Thus, he calls for licensing in the legal profession to be eliminated and replaced by voluntary certification, completion of alternative legal education courses of study, and optional bar examinations. Given the low information costs of determining the quality of a lawyer, especially when a lawyer's quality can be assessed based on winning or losing cases, and the ease of providing information to potential consumers about an incompetent or unethical lawyer, the market would be allowed to determine the "signals" that prospective lawyers seek to acquire to develop and promote their practice. Of course, consumer protection laws would continue to exist and could be applied when a lawyer commits fraud.

Norris, Orr, and Timmons argue that the information asymmetries in the provision of medical care are sufficiently costly and difficult to overcome to warrant some regulatory oversight. But they also identify beneficial licensing reforms, such as granting healthcare professionals, including nurse practitioners and physicians' assistants, full practice authority, simplifying the requirements for a primary care license, and possibly replacing the licensing requirement for physicians with certification.

Barrios echoes the concern that information asymmetries in financial services may be difficult to overcome. But he also identifies beneficial licensing reforms. For accountants, these reforms include revising educational requirements, streamlining the CPA examination process, increasing transparency for licensing agencies, and promoting voluntary certification. For financial advisors the proposed reforms include adopting fiduciary standards, streamlining regulatory oversight, and enhancing coordination and accountability between regulatory bodies.

Finally, all of the authors point out how new technologies could positively impact the practice of the leading professions, which could influence their licensing. Winston notes that artificial intelligence (AI) could have a significant effect on improving the efficiency of legal practice and possibly provide incentives for the legal industry to deregulate itself as lawyers engage in evolving technological competition and must integrate professionals with an AI and other intellectual backgrounds into the legal profession. Similarly, Norris, Orr, and Timmons indicate that AI and Large Language Models (LLMs) have the potential to greatly increase the productivity of physicians while changing their tasks to guiding AI or LLM through the diagnostic process. It will be important for licensing in the medical profession to evolve with rather than compromise new technologies. Barrios highlights that technology could increase transparency in financial services, making regulation less burdensome while improving compliance.

* * *

Both the share of workers in the United States that are required to have a license from a government agency to perform their jobs legally and the costs of occupational licensing have grown substantially in recent decades, but government policymakers have yet to show much interest in reducing those costs. By detailing how occupational licensing has created significant costs in the leading professions, this book hopes to attract the attention of other scholars and practitioners who advocate reforming those professions and policymakers who would hopefully be incentivized to play a constructive role to help implement the appropriate licensing reforms that we have outlined here.

5 CONCLUSIONS 153

By embracing market forces and new technologies, the proposed reforms could yield significant social benefits, improving the efficiency and productivity of the leading professions and setting a precedent for other occupations to adopt constructive licensing reforms. At the same time, the proposed reforms could create a more flexible, accessible, and equitable regulatory environment.

Index

Figures, notes, and tables are indicated by f, n, and t following page numbers

A
ABA. *See* American Bar Association
ABA Journal, 26
abortion rights, 47, 56–57
Abramova, Inna, 128
access to financial services, 143
access to legal services, 16–29
   criticisms of deregulating legal profession and, 23–29
   deregulation and increase in, 10, 61–62, 62n62, 63n63, 64–65
   entry deregulation and, 18–23, 22n17
   socioeconomic status and, 10, 18, 22, 22n17, 28, 34, 63n63, 65
   technological innovation and, 20n14, 34, 65–66
access to medical services
   emergency services and, 98
   health outcomes and, 78–80, 92
   licensing requirements and, 80–82, 91–95, 104
   physician shortage and, 78–79, 92–93, 98, 103–104
   in rural areas, 92, 98
accounting education programs
   as barrier to entry, 123–124
   history of, 116–118
   150-hour rule for, 116n4, 123–129, 125f, 125n8, 127f, 151
   proposed revisions to, 131–134, 132n10, 132t
   reduced number of students choosing, 114
   voluntary specialized certifications, 136–137
Accreditation Council on Graduate Medical Education (ACGME), 79, 89–90, 96–97
advanced practice registered nurses (APRNs), 98
affirmative action programs, 29n24
AI. *See* artificial intelligence

155

AICPA (American Institute of Certified Public Accountants), 117–118, 124, 125n8
Airline Deregulation Act (1974), 64n65
airline industry, 30, 64, 64n65
Alito, Samuel, Jr., 46n44, 48, 52
Allen Overy, 14
AMA (American Medical Association), 79, 84, 87, 91, 93–94
American Bar Association (ABA)
  accreditation of law schools, 9, 11–12, 11n2, 12n5, 15, 42, 45, 62n62
  discipline of lawyers' conduct, 25
  law practices, ownership requirements for, 14, 19–20
  Model Rules of Professional Conduct, 9, 13–14n8, 19–20, 28
  role of, 9
American Board of Medical Specialties, 83
American Institute of Certified Public Accountants (AICPA), 117–118, 124, 125n8
American Medical Association (AMA), 79, 84, 87, 91, 93–94
amicus curiae briefs, 57, 59
Am Law 200 (top 200 American Law Firms), 39n36
Angie's List (now Angi), 27
antitrust policies, 31, 38–41, 39nn35–36, 53n55
Appelbaum, Binyamin, 53n55
apprenticeship programs
  for accountants, 131, 131
  for lawyers, 11n2, 63n63
  residency programs for physicians, 89–91, 96–97, 101
APRNs (advanced practice registered nurses), 98

Arizona: Arizona Lawyer Apprentice Program, 63n63
  legal aid lawyers in, 22
  nonlawyer ownership of law firms in, 19n11, 63n63
Arlen, Jennifer, 10n1
Arons, Marilyn, 21n15
Arrow, Kenneth, 95–96
artificial intelligence (AI)
  CPA training and, 133
  legal practice efficiency and, 32–34, 152
  legal practice regulatory reform and, 65–66, 66n68
  medical diagnoses and, 103, 152
Ash, Elliott, 53, 57
AskMeHelpDesk.com, 21n15
asset-to-liability ratios, 121
assistant physicians, 101
Association of Professional Responsibility Lawyers, 13–14n8
attorneys. *See* lawyers and legal profession
AVVO, 27
Axiom Global and Counsel, 19n11

B

Balanced Budget Act (1997), 90
bar exams. *See* state bar examinations
Barrett, Amy Coney, 47n45, 48, 49
Barrios, John M., 111, 123, 126–128, 130, 150, 152
Barton, Benjamin H., 62n62
Baum, Lawrence, 46
Bazelon, Emily, 59
Behnke, Michelle, 67n69
Berrey, Ellen, 25, 25
Bibas, Stephen, 62n62
Biden, Joe
  access to legal services, increasing, 22n17

antitrust enforcement, 39
code of conduct for US Supreme
  Court justices, 67
eviction moratorium, 58n61
Jackson as US Supreme Court
  nominee of, 47n45
on presidential immunity decision,
  48
special commission on US Supreme
  Court, 52–53n55
Big Four accounting firms, 19
Big Tech, 38–39
Blair, Peter Q., 82
blockchain technology, 143
bonding mechanisms, 120
Bonica, Adam, 50, 51n52
Bork, Robert, 48
Bowie, Nikolas, 54, 58
Breyer, Stephen, 47n45, 64n65
broker-dealers, 114–115, 121–122.
  See also accounting and financial
  advising professions
Burk, David, 51
business consulting practices, 19–20
business degrees, 31–32
Butler, Paul, 17

C
California
  airline industry deregulation, 64
  apprenticeship programs for lawyers,
    11n2
  medical licensing in, 93
  Paraprofessional Program Working
    Group, 64
  regulation of title of "doctor", 83
Cape Fear (film), 26n22
Capitalism and Freedom (Friedman),
  2
capital markets. *See* accounting and
  financial advising professions

capture theory of regulation, 8, 62
Carroll, Sidney L., 17
Casey, Planned Parenthood v. (1992),
  47
Cassens Weiss, Debra, 21n15, 26
CEOs, training of, 31–32
Certified Public Accountants (CPAs).
  See accounting and financial
  advising professions
Chan, David C., Jr., 85n3
ChatGPT, 32–33, 65, 103
Chemerinsky, Erwin, 47n45, 49
Chen, Yiqun, 85n3
childbirth, 85, 94
children
  access to healthcare, 92
  legal representation of, 18, 20
Choi, Jonathan H., 32
Chung, Bobby W., 82
Clifford Chance, 14
Cohen, Alma, 50, 51n52
collaborative practice agreements
  between care providers and
  physicians, 98
competition
  in accounting and financial advising
    professions, 113–114, 113n2,
    128, 144
  antitrust policies and, 38–40
  corporation- and foreign-owned
    firms to increase, 19
  culture of law firms and, 44
  deregulation to increase, 3–4
  for law school students, 45
  in legal profession, 16, 61, 62n62,
    95n5
  medical licenses and reduction of,
    82, 84–85, 93–94
  for medical school applicants, 100
  occupational licensing and
    reduction of, 2, 3
  for residency programs, 90

state medical boards limiting, 95–96
conflicts of interest, 120, 139
Congress
  eviction moratorium and, 58n61
  expert panels for, 58–59
  lobbying by medical boards, 95–96
  overrepresentation of lawyers in, 34–35
  US Supreme Court's dominance of lawmaking by, 58
Consumer Protection Rule, 121
consumer-rights laws, 26
consumers. *See also* access to legal services; access to medical services; information asymmetry
  antitrust policy enforcement and welfare of, 38–40
  financial advice, seeking, 119–120, 139, 142–143
  influence on lawyers' behavior, 26
  medical licensing requirements and reduced access to care, 91–92
  negative effects of occupational licensing for, 2–4, 17
  residency hours and error rates, 96–97
  reviews from, 3, 27, 81
  self-representing litigant, 17
Continuing Professional Education (CPE), 118
contract review, 20, 29, 33
corporate law, judges' biases in, 50–51
corporate ownership of law practices, 16, 18–19
cost–benefit analyses, 37, 49n49, 50n50, 128
Cotton, Michele, 65
CPA examination
  history of, 117–118
  150-hour rule and reduction in exam candidates, 126–127, 127f
  passing rates for, 116n5
  proposed reforms to, 134–135
  public reporting of pass rates, 135
  required score for, 116
CPE (Continuing Professional Education), 118

D

Dagan, Hanoch, 10n1
Darrow, Clarence, 15
data scientists and engineers, 34
DEA (Drug Enforcement Administration), 83
Deese, Brian, 38
Defense Department, 45
DeFond, M., 115–116
Delaware Supreme Court on legal representation in eviction cases, 63
Deloitte, 19, 33
Deming, David J., 21n16
democracy, 44
Democratic-appointed judges, 50
dentistry, 17, 94
Devins, Neal, 46
disbarment, 26
discovery documents, 33
discrimination. *See* race and racism
Distributed Ledger Technology, 142
diversity recruitment initiatives, 29n24
Dobbs v. Jackson Women's Health Organization (2022), 47, 56–57
doctors. *See* medical profession
Dodd-Frank Act (2010), 114, 121, 138
DoNotPay, 66n68
Drug Enforcement Administration (DEA), 83
drug prescriptions, 83

E

Economic Analysis Group of Justice Department, 39–40
economics and economists
 capture theory of regulation and, 8
 on expert panels, 53–59
 federal judges, economics course for, 53
 ideological biases of, 55–56
 information asymmetry in medical services, 80–81
 legal licensing and, 15–17, 22
 legal services as credence good, 26–27, 26n22
 legal silos of information and knowledge of, 10–11n1
 medical profession compensation rates and shortages, 79
 monopoly prevention, 3
 on occupational licensing and employment reductions, 82
 opposition to occupational licensing, 2
 policymaking and, 38–40
education. *See* accounting education programs; law school; medical training programs
electricians, 17
ElevateNext, 19n11
emergency care, 98
energy industry, 8, 30
Engstrom, David Freeman, 63n63
Epstein, Lee, 50–51
Epstein, Richard, 51
Ernst and Young, 19
E.S.M. Securities, Florida, 124
Ethics
 ABA Model Rules of Professional Conduct, 9, 13–14n8, 19–20, 28
 accounting and financial management standards, 117, 118, 123, 141–142
 corporate ownership of law practices and, 16, 62
 medical licensing and, 93
Europe
 combined law degree programs in, 20–21
 medical licensing requirements in, 83–84, 88–89, 104
 physicians per capita in, 78–79
 physician training in, 95, 99
Eviction
 Delaware Supreme Court on legal representation in eviction cases, 63
 moratorium, 58n61
examinations for licensure, 2. *See also* CPA examination; state bar examinations
ex-offenders, 3, 16–17
expert panels, 46, 52–60, 53n55

F

Farranato, Chiara, 27
Federal Trade Commission (FTC), 39–41, 39n35
Federation of State Medical Boards (FSMB), 88
Feldstein, Paul, 100
fiduciary responsibility, 120, 137–138
fiduciary standards, 139–141
financial advising profession. *See* accounting and financial advising professions
Financial Industry Regulatory Authority (FINRA), 121–122, 138, 141
FinTech innovations, 142–143
First Amendment, 65, 65n66
fixed vs. growth mindsets, 37n34

Flexner Report (1911), 87, 94
Flood, John, 33
Florida
 CPA licensure in, 124
 law students acting as public defenders, 18
Florida Public Defenders Organization, 18
folk medicine, 81, 86–87, 87n4
foreign law firms, 14–15, 61–62
foreign-trained physicians, 90, 96
fraud, 121–122
Freshfields Bruckhaus Deringer, 14
Friedman, Milton
 on legal profession, 15
 on medical profession, 84, 91, 94
 on occupational licensing, 2, 115, 116
FSMB (Federation of State Medical Boards), 88
FTC (Federal Trade Commission), 39–41, 39n35

G
Gallop, 47
Gaston, Robert J., 17
geographic restrictions
 accountant licensing an, 118
 foreign law firms in United States, 14–15, 19, 61–62
 legal licensing and, 13–14n8, 13n6, 17, 61
 medical licensing and, 88–90, 93, 96
 occupational licensing and, 3
Georgetown University, 35
Georgia
 legal aid lawyers in, 22
 state supreme court on lieutenant governor election anomalies, 50

Glass-Steagall Act (1933), 122
Goodman, Joshua, 21n16, 21n16
Gorsuch, Neil, 48, 62n62, 65
government-employed lawyers, 40–45, 40–41n40
government policy. *See also* occupational licensing
 deregulation of legal profession and effect on, 34–42
 economic analyses of, 38
 failures of, 35–36
 lawyers' influence in, 9, 15, 34–35, 64, 150
 legal profession, states' regulatory reform in, 63–65, 63n63
 medical associations' and boards' influence in, 79, 82, 95–96
 over-regulation through proliferation of laws and regulations, 36–37
Great Depression, 117, 122
growth vs. fixed mindsets, 37n34

H
Hadfield, Gillian K., 32
H&R Block, proposed merger with TaxAct, 40
Hann, Rebecca N., 130
Harris, Barnett J., 21n15
Health and Human Services Department, 92
healthcare. *See* medical profession
health insurance, 78, 91, 92
Health Professional Shortage Areas (HPSAs), 92, 98
HelloPrenup, 20n14
Hemel, Daniel, 59–60
Henderson, Todd, 31–32
Henderson, William, 31
Hirschman, Albert O., 26
Holmes, Oliver Wendell, Jr., 59
Hopkins, Johns, 87

Howard, Philip K., 36–37
Howarth, Joan, 62n62

I
Idaho
 pharmacists, prescriptive authority of, 98
 telemedicine in, 88
IDEA (Individuals with Disabilities Education Act, 1990), 21n15
IMLC (Interstate Medical Licensure Compact), 88, 93
Incompetence
 of accountants, 116
 of financial advisors, 119, 141
 of lawyers, 16, 25–27, 26n22, 62, 62n62
 occupational licensing and protection from, 3
 of physicians, 81, 93, 96
Indiana, regulation of title of "doctor" in, 83
indigent adults, legal representation of, 18, 20
Individuals with Disabilities Education Act of 1990 (IDEA), 21n15
information asymmetry
 in accounting services, 112–113, 15, 152
 in financial advising services, 119–120, 152
 information technology and reduction in, 3, 27
 as justification for occupational licensing, 2
 in legal services, 15–16, 26–27, 151
 market failure and, 3
 in medical care, 80–82, 94, 102, 151
Infrastructure Investment and Jobs Act (2022), 36

innovation. *See* technological innovation
international law firm mergers, 14–15
internships. *See* apprenticeship programs
Interstate Medical Licensure Compact (IMLC), 88, 93
Investment Advisers Act (1940), 120
investment banking, 119, 122

J
Jackson, Ketanji Brown, 47n45
Jdinteractive (online degree), 12n5
Jones, Edith H., 50n50
judges, effect of deregulation of legal profession on, 46–60. *See also* Supreme Court, US
Justice Department, 39–40

K
Kansas Legal Services, 18
Kantner, Jonathan, 39
Kardashian, Kim, 11n2
Karpilow, Quentin, 3
Katz, Michael L., 58
Kavanaugh, Brett, 48
Khan, Lina, 38–39, 39n35
Kirkland and Ellis, 14
Klain, Ron, 58n61
Kleiner, Morris M., 16–17, 94
Knake, Renee Newman, 62n62
Knowles Myers, Caitlin, 56n58
Know Your Customer (KYC) requests, 142
KPMG, 19, 19
Kreitner, Roy, 10n1
Kronman, Anthony T., 66
Kudrle, Robert T., 17, 94

L
Landes, William, 51

162 INDEX

Large Language Models (LLMs), 103, 152
Laski, Harold, 59
Latham and Watkins, 14
law license. *See also* lawyers and legal profession; state bar examinations
  as barrier to competition, 62n62
  for paraprofessionals, 63n63, 64
  regulatory reform for, 61, 63n63
  requirement to practice la, 29
law practices
  AI and technological advances, 32–34, 32n25
  Am Law 200 and industry revenue, 39n36
  corporate ownership, ethics of, 16
  culture of, 44
  deregulation, effect on, 31–33
  diversity recruitment initiatives, 29n24
  management of, 31–32, 32n26
  ownership requirements for, 14–15, 14n9, 19–20, 19n11, 63n63, 64
  poaching government-employed lawyers, 41
law school
  ABA accreditation requirements, 9, 11–12, 11n2, 12n5, 15, 42, 45, 62n62
  combined degree programs, 20–21, 20n13, 32n26
  cost of, 12, 20–21, 25
  culture of, 30–31
  deregulation and outcomes for, 22–23
  as entry barrier to legal profession, 11–12, 20, 20n13, 151
  internships and, 35, 35
  LSAT for admittance to, 11, 11n3, 20n13, 28–29
  multidisciplinary approaches to teaching, 30–31, 42–45, 42n41, 43n42
  online, 12n5, 21n16
  regulatory reform for, 61
  requirements for licensure, 9, 15
  return on investment, 24–25
  US News and World Report rankings, 28–29
  US Supreme Court clinics at top-tier schools, 60
  US Supreme Court justices learning ideological instincts in, 49–50
Law School Admission Council, 20n13
Law School Admission Test (LSAT), 11, 11n3, 20n13, 28–29
lawyers and legal profession, 74–75. *See also* access to legal services; law practices; state bar associations; state bar examinations
  barriers to entry, 9–17, 18–23, 20n13, 42–45, 151
  compensation rates, 12, 17–18, 19n12, 24–25, 25n20, 40
  cost and access to services, 10, 16–29, 22n17, 62n62, 63n63, 64–65
  criticisms of deregulation, 23–29
  deregulation, effect on judges, 46–60
  deregulation, effect on lawyers, 10, 29–45
  ethics and ABA Model Rules of Professional Conduct, 9, 13–14n8, 19–20, 28
  geographic restrictions on licensure, 13–14n8, 13n6, 17, 61
  government-employed lawyers, 40–45, 40–41n40

government policy, influence in, 9, 15, 34–35, 64, 150
lawyers as government policymakers, 34–42
licensing effects on, 1–5
overview, 8–10
in private practice, 31–34
regulatory reform for, 60–68
Utah and waivers of state's unauthorized practice of law rules, 11n2
Lazarus, Richard J., 54
Leffler, Keith, 82
legal aid lawyers, 22
legal externships, 23
legal paraprofessionals, 63n63, 64
legal research and development, 33
Legal Services Corporation, 22
Legal Services Link, 34
LegalZoom, 20, 62n62
Leonard, Jennifer, 32n25
Levine, Michael, 64n65
Liaison Committee for Graduate Medical Education, 89. *See also* Accreditation Council on Graduate Medical Education
life expectancy rates, 92
Lincoln, Abraham, 15
Linklaters, 14
Litan, Robert E., 8
litigation and regulatory reform, 65–66
LLMs (Large Language Models), 103, 152
lobbying, 82, 95–96, 125n9
Lola v. Skadden (2015), 65–66
LSAT (Law School Admission Test), 11, 11n3, 20n13, 28–29

M

Maine, legal apprenticeship programs in, 11n2

major questions doctrine, 48
Maloney Act (1938), 122
malpractice insurance, 17, 83, 91, 96, 102
Manne Economics Institute, 53
market forces. *See also* competition
credence goods and information technology, 27
deregulation and competition, 3–4
medical licensing reforms based on, 97–102
natural monopolies and failure of, 3
Marshall, John, 15
Martindale-Hubbell, 27
Massachusetts, bar examination in, 15
Master of Business Administration (MBA), 31–32
McDonald, R. Robin, 50
McKinsey, 33
Medical College Admission Test (MCAT), 93
medical profession, 77–110. *See also* access to medical services; medical training programs
barriers to entry, 79–82, 79n1, 94, 151
compensation rates for physicians, 79, 82
in Europe vs. United States, 83–84, 88–89, 104
foreign residency training and, 90, 96
FSMB establishment and geographic mobility, 88–89
geographic restrictions on, 88–90, 93, 96
history of medical licensing, 85–88
licensing costs, 89, 91, 93, 101
licensing effects on, 1–5
low-cost alternatives to services, 27–28

market-oriented reforms and regulations, 97–102
negatives of licensing on access and quality, 91–95
overview of licensing, 83–83
physician self-interested behavior and, 82, 95–97
qualifications for, 81
residency requirements, 89–91
shortage of physicians, 78–82, 92–93, 98, 103–104
technology and market disruption, 103
medical training programs
accreditation of, 79
AMA influence in, 79
as barrier to entry, 94
in Europe vs. United States, 95, 99
MCAT exams, 93
obstetricians and restrictions on midwifery, 85, 94
residency training, 79, 89–91, 96–97, 101, 104
shorter and combined programs, 95, 99–101, 104, 151
student loan debt and, 82, 99
Medicare, 90, 91–92
mergers and acquisitions, 39n36, 40, 128
Michaels, Dave, 40
midwives, 85, 94
Miller, Joe, 29n24
Miller, Sarah, 56n58
minimum wage, 55, 55n57
Minnesota, CPA educational reforms in, 132n7
minorities. *See* race and racism
Mississippi, legal aid lawyers in, 22
monopolies, 3, 16, 36, 86, 102
Montana, prescriptive authority of pharmacists in, 98

N

National Association of Assistant United States Attorneys (NAAUSA), 40–41n40
National Association of Securities Dealers (NASD), 122
National Association of State Boards of Accountancy (NASBA), 118, 135
National Center for State Courts, 17
National Economic Council, 39
National Intern Matching Program (now National Resident Matching Program), 89
naturopaths, 87n4
NBME-Free-Step-1, 103
negligence of physicians, 81, 96–97
Net Capital Rule (1975), 121
New York
attorney competence study in, 25
corporation- and foreign-owned firms in, 19
legal aid lawyers in New York City, 22
panel attorney compensation rates in, 18
UPL and First Amendment rights violations, 65
New York Stock Exchange (NYSE), 122
Nitze, Jane, 62n62
Nixon, Richard, 48
Norris, Conor, 77, 150–152
nurse practitioners (NPs), 85, 85n3, 98, 104, 151

O

occupational licensing. *See also* accounting and financial advising professions; lawyers and legal profession; medical profession
benefits and justifications for, 2

costs of, 150–153
defined, 1
as entry barrier to professional services, 1–4
negative effects of, 2–4, 9–10
Office of the Solicitor General, 41
Oklahoma
  CPA licensure in, 124, 125n9
  public defender compensation rates in, 18
online education, 12n5, 21n16, 62
Oregon, Supervised Practice Portfolio Examination, 11n2
Organisation for Economic Co-operation and Development (OECD), physicians per capita in, 78–79
originalism, 48–49
Orr, Robert, 77, 150–152
Osler, William, 87
osteopaths, 87n4

P

Packel, Dan, 63n63
Pagliero, Mario, 95n5
Pakaluk, Catherine, 56–57
panel attorneys, 18
Paralegals, 28
PAs (physician assistants), 85, 98, 151
Peltzman, Sam, 8, 62, 82
Penn Square Bank, Oklahoma, 124
pharmacists, 98
physician assistants (PAs),, 85, 98, 104, 151
physicians. *See* medical profession; medical training programs
Planned Parenthood v. Casey (1992), 47
plea deals, 17–18
police brutality, 22
political polarization, 46–47

Posner, Richard
  on access to legal services, 22n17
  on amicus briefs, 57
  on expert panels as beneficial to US Supreme Court policy-based decisions, 52
  on finding legal arguments to justify decisions, 57, 58n61
  on information silos in legal profession, 10–11n1
  on motivated thinking of US Supreme Court justices, 54
  on Supreme Court justices' ideological behavior, 49, 51
Precedent
  in *Dobbs* case, 47
  evading, 54–55
  personal precedent of Supreme Court justice, 52n53
  policy inefficiencies and, 37
  on presidential immunity, 48
prenuptial agreements, 20n14
prescriptive authority, 83, 98
presidential election (2020), 66
presidential immunity, 47–48
PricewaterhouseCoopers, 19
principal-agent relationships, 119. *See also* accounting and financial advising professions
pro bono services, 22, 34
professional associations, 2. *See also specific associations*
professionalism, 95, 113
pro se litigants, 17
public defenders, 18
Pyle, Mark, 38

Q

quality of life. *See also* access to legal services; access to medical services
  access to financial services and, 143
  access to professionals and, 4

disease and life expectancy, 92
regulation enforcement and, 37
Roe v. Wade and, 56

R

race and racism
   barriers to legal profession and, 15
   CPA educational requirements and, 128
   diversity recruitment initiatives and, 29n24
   economic effects of abortion and, 56
   examination scores and, 28
   medical schools and, 87–88
   Republican- vs. Democrat-appointed judges, sentencing bias of, 50
railroad industry, 30
Re, Richard M., 52n53
Reagan, Ronald, 53n55
regulation. *See* government policy; occupational licensing
Regulation Best Interest (2018), 122
Regulation M, 122, 122n7
Regulation SHO, 122, 122n7
regulatory capture
   in accounting and financial advising professions, 113
   in legal profession, 8, 35, 62
Rehnquist, William, 51
Republican-appointed judges, 50
Reputation
   credence goods and, 26–27
   deregulation and information availability, 26
   information technology and increased visibility of, 3, 27
Residency Review Committees (RRCs), 89
residency training, 79, 89–91, 96–97, 101, 104
reviews
   consumer demand based on, 3, 27
   information asymmetry in medical services, 81
Reynolds, Matt, 33
Rhode, Deborah L., 25
Rittenhouse, Kyle, 17–18
Robb, Lachlan, 33
Roberts, John, 48, 50–51
Roe v. Wade (1973), 47, 56
Rozema, Kyle, 12–13, 25, 26n21
rural areas
   access to legal services and, 63n63
   access to medical care and, 92, 98

S

St. Mary's University School of Law, 12n5
savings and loan crisis (1980s), 124
Schrager, Allison, 38
Schwarcz, Daniel, 32
scope of practice, 83, 97–98
Scott, Robert E., 10n1
Securities Act (1933), 117, 120
Securities and Exchange Commission (SEC). *See also specific regulations*
   creation of, 117, 120
   on decline in registered broker-dealers, 114, 138
   private law firms hiring lawyers from, 41
   regulatory oversight of, 120–122, 138, 141
Securities Exchange Act (1934), 117, 120–122
self-capture, 9, 60
self-regulatory organizations (SROs), 121–122
self-representing litigants, 17
Sen, Maya, 50, 51n52
Series 65 exam for securities market, 121

INDEX

Shapiro, Carl, 39
Shearman and Sterling, 14
Sidley Austin, 13
Simon, Michael, 65
small-claims court, 20
Smith, Adam, 2
Smith, Patrick, 32n25
social media reviews, 27
socioeconomic status
   income redistribution policies, 36
   law school costs and, 20–21
   legal services access and, 10, 18, 22, 22n17, 28, 34, 63n63, 65
   medical care access and, 80, 92
   policy failures and,, 36
Solicitor General's Office, 59
Sotomayor, Sonia, 47
South Carolina, CPA educational reforms in, 132n7
special masters, 53
SROs (self-regulatory organizations), 121–122
state bar associations
   admission without going to law school, 11n2
   discipline of lawyers' conduct, 25, 26, 26n21
   First Amendment rights violations and, 65n66
state bar examinations
   alternatives to, 11n2
   Arizona Lawyer Apprentice Program and, 63n63
   ChatGPT passing, 32–33
   consumer protection from incompetence, 3
   difficulty increased to limit competition, 95n5
   as entry barrier to legal profession, 9, 12–13
   licensure of those attending state's flagship law school, 25–26
   quality standards and, 15
   Washington state waiver, 63n63
State Boards of Accountancy, 117
state legislators
   as lawyers and thus self-regulating legal profession, 9
   legal profession reform initiated by, 63–65, 63n63
   medical board oversight and, 95
state medical boards
   consumer protection through oversight, 96–97, 104
   FSMB, establishment of, 88–89
   licensure and discipline from, 79, 91, 93, 96
   limiting competition, 95–96
   simplified licensing recommendations, 100–101
Stevens, John Paul, 50
Stigler-Peltzman capture theory of regulation, 8
stockbrokers, 122. *See also* Securities and Exchange Commission
Strohl, Jeff, 25n20
student loan debt, 25n20, 82, 99
Supreme Court, US
   on abortion rights, 47, 56–57
   on affirmative action programs, 29n24
   code of conduct rules, 67
   on eviction moratorium, 58n61
   expert panels, use of, 46, 52–60, 53n55
   ideological polarity, evidence of, 50–52, 51n52, 52–53n55
   justices' ideological behavior, 46–50, 47n45, 49n49, 150
   law school clinics on, 60
   objections to expert panels, 54–60
   on presidential immunity, 47–48
   proposed reforms for, 59–60, 67
   public approval ratings for, 47

Sutherland, A. G., 128
Sweden, medical licensing in, 83–84, 84n2
Syracuse University College of Law, 12n5

T
tariffs, 38
TaxAct, proposed merger with H&R Block, 40
technological innovation. *See also* Artificial intelligence
  CPA training and, 133
  credence goods, assessing value of, 27
  deregulation and incentives for, 29–30
  deregulation of legal profession and, 10, 32–34, 32n25
  in FinTech, 142–143, 152
  information asymmetries, reduction in, 3, 27
  lawyers, assessing quality of, 16
  legal profession regulatory reform and, 65–66
  medical practice disruption and, 103
  online education, 12n5, 21n16, 62
  physicians, assessing quality of, 93, 102
  service offerings and consumer welfare, 8, 20
  telemedicine and, 88
telecommunications industry, 8, 30
telemedicine, 88
Texas
  Access to Justice Commission, 63n63
  airline industry deregulation, 64
  state bar association and First Amendment rights violations, 65n66

Thomas, Clarence, 48
Thompson, Neil C., 53n56
Timmons, Edward, 77, 150–152
Triantis, George D., 10n1
Tribe, Laurenc, 58n61
Trillion Dollar Economist (Litan), 8
trucking industry, 8, 30
Trump, Donald
  criminal offenses of, 37
  delay of criminal trials, 66
  tariffs and inflation, 38
Tsai Leadership Program, Yale Law School, 43n42
Turnaway Study, 56n58
TurnSignl (mobile app), 34

U
unauthorized practice of law (UPL), 9, 21n15, 26, 63n63, 65–66, 66n68
Uniform Accountancy Act (UAA, 1992), 118
uniform bar exam (UBE), 13, 32–33
Uniform CPA Examination. *See* CPA examination
University of Virginia Law School, 20n13
Upsolve, 65
USC Gould School of Law, 20n13
US News and World Report rankings of law schools, 28–29
Utah waivers of unauthorized practice of law rules, 63n63

V
Vance, JD, 38
Vermuele, Adrian, 48
Veterans Benefits Administration, 37
Villasenor, John, 43n42
virtual briefings, 53

voluntary certifications of accounting professionals, 136–137
Vorotnikov, Evgeny S., 16–17

W

Ward, Stephanie Francis, 63n63
Washington, DC
 law internships with government lawmakers, 35
 nonlawyer ownership of law firms in, 14n9
Washington state waiver of bar examination, 63n63
Wealth of Nations (Smith), 2
Welch, Morgan, 56n58
Welch, William, 87
West Virginia v. Environmental Protection Agency (2022), 48
Wikipedia, 53n56
Wilson, Christine, 39n35
Winston, Clifford, 1, 7, 149
 on antitrust legal cases, 40–41
 on entry barriers to legal profession, 17, 150–152
 on ideological polarity of Supreme Court Justices, 51
 on occupational licensing and protection from incompetence, 3
 on return on law school education, 24–25
Wisconsin, practicing law without bar exam in, 11n2
Wu, Tim, 38–39

Y

Yale Law School, 43n42
Yan, Jia, 51
Yang, Crystal S., 50
Yelp, 27

Z

Zhang, J., 115–116

Printed in the United States
by Baker & Taylor Publisher Services